MW00437660

THE BOOK OF
BIBLE
PROMISES

RON RHODES

HARVEST HOUSE PUBLISHERS

EUGENE, OREGON

Unless otherwise indicated, all Scripture quotations are taken from the HOLY BIBLE, NEW INTERNATIONAL VERSION®. NIV®. Copyright©1973, 1978, 1984 by the International Bible Society. Used by permission of Zondervan. All rights reserved.

Verses marked NASB are taken from the New American Standard Bible®, © 1960, 1962, 1963, 1968, 1971, 1972, 1973, 1975, 1977, 1995 by The Lockman Foundation. Used by permission.

Verses marked KJV are taken from the King James Version of the Bible.

Cover by Dugan Design Group, Bloomington, Minnesota

Cover photo © Jason Verschoor / iStockphoto

THE BOOK OF BIBLE PROMISES

Copyright © 2003/2009 by Ron Rhodes
Published by Harvest House Publishers
Eugene, Oregon 97402
www.harvesthousepublishers.com

Library of Congress Cataloging-in-Publication Data
    Rhodes, Ron.
    [Complete book of Bible promises]
    The book of Bible promises / Ron Rhodes.
        p. cm.
    Originally published: The complete book of Bible promises. Eugene, Or. : Harvest House, 2003.
    ISBN 978-0-7369-2346-0 (pbk.)
    1. God—Promises—Biblical teaching. 2. Promise (Christian theology)—Biblical teaching. I. Title.
    BS680.P68R48 2009
    231.7—dc22
                                                                    2008032939

All rights reserved. No part of this publication may be reproduced, stored in a retrieval system, or transmitted in any form or by any means—electronic, mechanical, digital, photocopy, recording, or any other—except for brief quotations in printed reviews, without the prior permission of the publisher.

Printed in China

09 10 11 12 13 14 15 / RDS-SK / 10 9 8 7 6 5 4 3 2 1

To the glory of our faithful God,
who has "given us his very great
and precious promises."

2 PETER 1:4

Acknowledgments

Scripture proclaims that a good wife is "worth far more than rubies" (Proverbs 31:10), and that children are a gift from God (Psalm 127:3). What a fortunate man I am to have a wonderful wife, Kerri, and two wonderful children, David and Kylie. What did I ever do to deserve such blessing? As I write these words, I remember that this God of promises of whom Scripture speaks delights in giving us that which we do not deserve. Truly, God is ultimately deserving of praise and thanks for His wonderful blessing. May His name be exalted (Psalm 57:5,11)!

Contents

Every time I hear the story, my heart swells in praise to God for His faithfulness.

Horatio Gates Spafford was a personal friend of the great evangelist Dwight Moody. Spafford and his family decided to go on a vacation. The plan was to go to England in November 1873 to join Moody and Ira Sankey on an evangelistic crusade and then travel in Europe. Spafford had to attend to some last-minute business before he could leave, so he sent his family on ahead on a great ship—a French steamer called the *Ville de Havre*.

Tragically, the ship never reached its destination. It collided with another ship off the coast of Newfoundland and quickly sank. Only 47 of the 226 passengers survived. One of these was Spafford's wife, Anna. Their four young daughters—Maggie, Tanetta, Annie, and Bessie—drowned and perished in the harsh, icy waters. I can hardly imagine what Spafford must have felt when he received a telegram from his bereaved wife saying, "Saved alone."

Spafford immediately dropped all business and sailed to Europe to be with his wife. Upon reuniting, they met with Moody. Spafford said to him, "It is well. The will of God be done."

Some time after this overwhelming personal tragedy, Spafford penned the words to one of the most beloved hymns in Christian history, "It Is Well with My Soul." The lyrics stir the soul:

When peace like a river attendeth my way;
When sorrows like sea billows roll;
Whatever my lot, Thou hast taught me to say,
It is well, it is well with my soul.

(refrain)
It is well with my soul,
It is well, it is well with my soul.

Though Satan should buffet, though trials should come,
Let this blest assurance control,
That Christ hath regarded my helpless estate,
And hath shed His own blood for my soul.

(refrain)

My sin—oh, the bliss of this glorious thought—
 My sin, not in part, but the whole,
Is nailed to the cross, and I bear it no more.
 Praise the Lord, praise the Lord, O my soul.

(refrain)

And, Lord, haste the day when our faith shall be sight,
 The clouds be rolled back as a scroll,
The trump shall resound, and the Lord shall descend;
 Even so, it is well with my soul.

(refrain)

Surely Spafford's profound words were inspired by the wonderful promises of God. They enabled him, despite devastating grief, to rest in the peace and comfort that only God can give. God is faithful!

You may be facing deep waters and bitter trials in your own life. Dear friend, turn to God and trust in His promises. Supernatural tranquility and peace are available to you in every situation. They are yours for the taking. Cast yourself on God and His promises—and truly trust in Him—and this peace will be yours. He will sustain you. God is faithful!

Never forget that our God is a promise keeper. Numbers 23:19 asserts, "God is not a man, that he should lie, nor a son of man, that he should change his mind. Does he speak and then not act? Does he promise and not fulfill?" Prior to his death, an aged Joshua declared: "Now I am about to go the way of all the earth. You know with all your heart and soul that not one of all the good promises the Lord your God gave you has failed. Every promise has been fulfilled; not one has failed" (Joshua 23:14; see also Joshua 21:45). Solomon later proclaimed: "Praise be to the Lord, who has given rest to his people Israel just as he promised. Not one word has failed of all the good promises he gave through his servant Moses" (1 Kings 8:56). God truly is faithful!

The Blessedness of the Faith Life

The writer to the Hebrews defined faith as "being sure of what we hope for and certain of what we do not see" (Hebrews 11:1). The big problem for most people is that they tend to base everything on what the five senses reveal. And since the spiritual world is not subject to any of these, the faith of many people is often weak and impotent.

The eye of faith, however, perceives this unseen reality. The spiritual world is all around us, enclosing us, embracing us, altogether within our reach. God Himself is here awaiting our response to His presence—awaiting our response to His many promises. He is here to comfort us. We will become aware of the spiritual world the moment we begin to reckon upon its reality and believe what He has promised.

I often think about the story of Elisha in 2 Kings 6:8-23. Elisha was completely surrounded by enemy troops, yet he remained calm and relaxed. His servant, however, must have been climbing the walls at the sight of this hostile army with big, vicious-looking warriors and innumerable battle chariots on every side. (In my mind's eye, I picture this servant as being a Don Knotts type.) Undaunted, Elisha said to him: "Don't be afraid. Those who are with us are more than those who are with them" (6:16). Elisha then prayed to God, "'O

Lord, open his eyes so he may see.' Then the Lord opened the servant's eyes, and he looked and saw the hills full of horses and chariots of fire all around Elisha" (6:17). God was protecting Elisha and his servant with a whole army of magnificent angelic beings!

Elisha never got frazzled because he was "sure of what he hoped for and certain of what he did not see." Here was a man who believed that God would fulfill what He had promised. The eyes of faith can see God acting on our behalf even when our physical eyes cannot. The eyes of faith recognize that God is indeed a God of promises and that He will respond to those who come to Him in faith!

Conditioning the Faith Muscle

Great Christian thinkers have often commented that faith is like a muscle. A muscle has to be repeatedly stretched to the limit of its endurance in order to build more strength. Without increased stress in training, the muscle will simply not grow.

In the same way, faith must be repeatedly tested to the limit of its endurance in order to expand and develop. Very often, God allows His children to go through trying experiences in order to develop their faith muscles (1 Peter 1:7). God's children need to learn to trust in the promises He has made. This learning process takes place in the school of real life—with all of its difficult trials and tribulations.

The book of Exodus shows this process in action.

Following Israel's deliverance from Egypt, God first led them to Marah, a place where they would be forced to trust God to heal the water to make it drinkable. Significantly, God led them to Marah before leading them to Elim, a gorgeous oasis with plenty of good water (Exodus 15:22-27). God could have bypassed Marah altogether and brought them directly to Elim if He had wanted to. But, as is characteristic of God, He purposefully led them through the route that would yield maximum conditioning of their faith muscles, a route that forced them to trust in His promises of sustenance. God does the same type of thing with us. He often governs our circumstances so as to yield maximum conditioning of our faith muscles. God takes us through the school of hard knocks to teach us that He is reliable and that He indeed does faithfully follow through with His promises.

Faith and the Word of God

Without question, the Word of God can strengthen the faith of believers. John's Gospel proclaims that "these [things in John's Gospel] are written that you may believe" (John 20:31, insert added). Paul tells us that "faith comes from hearing the message, and the message is heard through the word of Christ" (Romans 10:17). If someone should ask, How can I increase my faith? the answer is, Saturate your mind with God's Word.

The more you know about the promises of God in the Word of God, the stronger your faith will be in appropriating them. Conversely, the less you know about the promises of God in His Word, the weaker your faith will be, and you will be ignorant of the vast and untapped reservoir of help that is available to you. No wonder the psalmist made a point of saying, "My eyes stay open through the watches of the night, that I may meditate on your promises" (Psalm 119:148).

My friend, I have compiled God's promises in this book so that...

- you may appropriate them in your life and enjoy the supernatural peace that goes along with trusting in these promises

- you may learn the lessons of faith and trust—and the accompanying blessings—that God has in store for you

May the Lord bless you mightily as you use this book!

═══ Recognizing the Promises of God ═══

If we are to place our faith in the promises of God, then at the outset, we must be sure what *is* and what *is not* a promise of God in the Bible. Obviously, if we claim a verse as a promise that is in fact not really a promise at all, then our faith is misplaced, and we will be disillusioned when we do not see the results we are looking for. We will not, however, be disappointed in God's Word so long as we interpret it correctly (2 Timothy 2:15) and claim as promises only those verses intended to be promises for us today.

On my bookshelf are a number of small paperback books containing "promises" of God. The problem is that many of the "promises" in these books are really not promises at all. For instance, one "promise" found in many of these books is 1 Thessalonians 4:9, found under the heading of "Brotherly Love": "Now about brotherly love we do not need to write to you, for you yourselves have been taught by God to love each other." In truth, this verse is simply affirming that the Thessalonian Christians have been taught by God to love one another. Nothing in this verse indicates that God is promising to do anything for believers. Claiming this verse as a promise is therefore a misuse of Scripture.

I could cite literally hundreds of such examples from

various books that are full of Bible "promises," but such an exercise might seem ungracious and overly critical. My only point is that we need to be clear regarding what is and what is not a Bible promise. Only then can we confidently put our assurance in the Word of God.

Toward this end, I suggest some basic principles for understanding what is and what is not a Bible promise. These are simple observations based on many years of studying God's Word.

1. Promises made to *specific* individuals are not intended to be promises for *all* believers. An example is Genesis 12:2: "I will bless you; I will make your name great, and you will be a blessing." This promise was made to Abraham alone, not to believers in general. Therefore, modern believers should not claim this as a Bible promise for themselves.

Another example is 2 Kings 20:6: "I will add fifteen years to your life." This promise was made to Hezekiah alone, not to all believers.

When we encounter promises in the Bible, a good question to ask is: "Who is this promise being made to? Does the context indicate that it is a promise that I can claim, or is it a promise for a specific individual?"

2. Promises made to Old Testament Israelites are generally not promises to people today. Numerous Old Testament promises were made specifically to the Israelites in a very specific context and cannot be properly claimed by modern believers. In the book of Deuteronomy, for example,

God through Moses promised great blessings if the theocratic (God-ruled) nation lived in obedience to the Sinaitic covenant God made with them. God also promised that if the nation disobeyed His commands, it would experience the punishments listed in the covenant—including exile from the land (Deuteronomy 28:15-68).

Old Testament history is replete with illustrations of how unfaithful Israel was to the covenant. The two most significant periods of exile for the Jewish people involved the fall of Israel to the Assyrians in 722 BC and the collapse of Judah to the Babylonians in 597–581 BC. As God promised, disobedience brought exile to God's own people.

A rather famous promise made to the Old Testament Israelites that is sometimes misappropriated today is 2 Chronicles 7:14: "If my people, who are called by my name, will humble themselves and pray and seek my face and turn from their wicked ways, then will I hear from heaven and will forgive their sin and will heal their land." These are words that God spoke specifically to Solomon regarding the Israelites (God's "my people" of the Old Testament), yet how often do we hear people today claiming this verse as a promise from God regarding the United States? Now, don't get me wrong. Aside from being a *specific promise* to Israel, we also find in this verse the *general principle* that God responds to prayer and humility by bringing about healing. Based on this *general principle*, citizens of the United States should humble themselves and pray and ask God for the healing of our land—but we cannot claim this verse as an ironclad promise for the United States. To put it another way, the *general principle* can apply to all people and all nations—and God may well heal a modern nation that humbles itself and prays—but the *ironclad promise* that was set in stone and was guaranteed to be fulfilled was made to Israel alone.

Let us remember that we are instructed to avoid distorting the Bible (2 Peter 3:16) and that we are called to correctly handle the word of truth (2 Timothy 2:15). Because many verses in the Old Testament deal specifically with the Israelites in specific contexts, we would misinterpret the Bible if we claimed some of the promises for ourselves that God made to them. But we can derive principles from such promises and apply these principles to our situations. So, for example, when we read a promise made to the Israelite nation that God would bless their obedience (Deuteronomy 28:2), we can derive the general principle that God blesses obedience, and base our lives on that principle.

3. *Some* Bible promises made in the Old Testament *are* applicable to today. This would include Bible promises based on God's nature and not on specific circumstances among the Israelites. An example of this is Isaiah 55:11, which makes reference to the effectiveness of God's Word: "It will not return to me empty, but will accomplish what I desire and achieve the purpose for which I sent it." This promise is based entirely on God's intrinsic sovereignty. Since the verse is based on God's nature (a nature that does not change), the verse speaks of something that is true at all times in all places. Therefore, we may rest assured that God's Word is still as effective today as it was in Old Testament times.

Some promises made in the Old Testament are applicable today because of strong parallel promises in the New Testament. Such parallels indicate that God issues certain general promises to His people, regardless of whether they lived in Old Testament times or New Testament times and beyond. An example is Psalm 34:22: "No one will be condemned who takes refuge in him." This rings quite similar to John 3:18, where we read, "Whoever believes in him is not condemned."

Further, some Old Testament promises of God are made to those who "trust in the Lord" or "take refuge in the Lord" or "hope in the Lord," which are applicable to Christians today who trust in the Lord, take refuge in Him, and hope in Him. For example, in Isaiah 40:31 we read, "Those who hope in the Lord will renew their strength. They will soar on wings like eagles; they will run and not grow weary, they will walk and not be faint." In Psalm 31:23 we read that "the Lord preserves the faithful." In Psalm 34:10 we read that "those who seek the Lord lack no good thing." Such general promises seem to belong to believers of all ages.

4. **"Wisdom sayings" in the book of Proverbs are not intended to be Bible promises.** The book of Proverbs is a "wisdom book" and contains maxims of moral wisdom. The maxims found in this book were engineered to help the

young in ancient Israel acquire mental skills that promote wise living.

The word *proverb* literally means "to be like," or "to be compared with." A proverb, then, is a form of communicating truth by using comparisons or figures of speech. The proverbs, in a memorable way, crystallize and condense the writers' experiences and observations about life, and provide general principles that are generally (but not always) true. The reward of meditating on these maxims or "wisdom sayings" is, of course, wisdom. But these maxims were never intended as Bible promises.

A verse often misconstrued as a promise is Proverbs 22:6: "Train a child in the way he should go, and when he is old he will not turn from it." I know of parents who have claimed this verse as a promise and have done everything they could to bring their children up rightly and in the fear of the Lord. But in some cases, the children have ended up departing from Christianity and going astray in life. The parents of these children became disillusioned and wondered what they did wrong. But Proverbs 22:6 was never intended to be a promise. Like other "wisdom sayings" in the book of Proverbs, this verse contains a general principle that is generally true. But a general principle always involves some exceptions to the rule. (Keep in mind that God Himself is the most perfect parent there is, but His children, Adam and Eve, certainly went astray.)

The good news is that if you follow the general principles laid out in the book of Proverbs, you will generally see certain positive results in your life, and your life will generally be much more successful! But principles are not the same as promises.

5. Words uttered by human beings that are recorded in Scripture are not necessarily Bible promises. Of course, the words of the prophets and apostles *do* contain many promises of God, and we should pay careful attention to these promises. But in other cases, Scripture simply records something that a particular human being (who was not a prophet or an apostle) said, and those words cannot be claimed as a promise. For example, in Job 4:8 we read: "Those who plow evil and those who sow trouble reap it." At first glance it might appear that God is promising to bring evil upon those who themselves cause evil. In context, however, these are words that Eliphaz the Temanite spoke to Job during his time of suffering. Therefore, these words do not constitute a promise of God. Likewise, in Job 8:6 we read: "If you are pure and upright, even now he will rouse himself on your behalf and restore you to your rightful place." Again, at first glance it might appear that God is here making a promise. But the context shows that these are words that Bildad the Shuhite spoke to Job. We must always be cautious not to claim as a promise of God something that a person spoke to another person.

6. Some Bible promises are unconditional, whereas others are conditional. This book contains both types of promises.

THE BOOK OF BIBLE PROMISES

A conditional promise is a promise with an "if" attached. This type of promise necessitates meeting certain obligations or conditions before God fulfills it. If God's people fail in meeting the conditions, God is not obligated in any way to fulfill the promise. An example is James 1:25: "The man who looks intently into the perfect law that gives freedom, and continues to do this, not forgetting what he has heard, but doing it—he will be blessed in what he does." The promised blessing in this verse hinges on obeying God's Word. Another example is John 15:7: "If you remain in me and my words remain in you, ask whatever you wish, and it will be given you." This promise guarantees answered prayer *only* for those in whom Christ's words remain and those who remain in Christ. So long as the conditions are met, the promise is fulfilled.

An unconditional promise depends on no such conditions for its fulfillment. No "ifs" are attached. That which is promised is sovereignly given to the recipient of the promise apart from the recipient's merit (or lack of it). Such promises are true for all who belong to the family of God. Many of the promises relating to the Christian's positional standing in Christ or the blessings we have in Christ are unconditional. For example, we read in Galatians 4:6-7, "Because you are sons, God sent the Spirit of his Son into our hearts, the Spirit who calls out, 'Abba, Father.' So you are no longer a slave, but a son; and since you are a son, God has made you also an heir." The fact that we are sons and heirs in God's family does not hinge on meeting certain conditions. Rather it is something that is true of all Christians.

7. **When interpreting the promises of God, always keep in mind what other Scriptures on the same subject reveal.** Scripture interprets Scripture. This principle says that if one interprets a particular verse in a way that clearly contradicts other Bible verses, then one's interpretation is incorrect. Scriptural harmony is essential. In view of this principle, consider the Bible promise in Mark 11:23-24: "I tell you the truth, if anyone says to this mountain, 'Go, throw yourself into the sea,' and does not doubt in his heart but believes that what he says will happen, it will be done for him. Therefore I tell you, whatever you ask for in prayer, believe that you have received it, and it will be yours."

We must interpret this promise in light of what other Scripture verses reveal. The broader context of Scripture places limitations on what God will give. God cannot literally give us anything. Some things are actually impossible for God to give. For example, God cannot grant a request of a creature to be God. Neither can He answer a request to approve of our sin. God will not give us a stone if we ask for bread, nor will He give us a snake if we ask for fish (Matthew 7:9-10).

Scripture places other conditions on God's promise to answer prayer in addition to faith. We must abide in Him and let His Word abide in us (John 15:7 KJV). We cannot "ask amiss" out of our own selfishness (James 4:3 KJV). Furthermore, we must ask "according to his will" (1 John 5:14).

We must ever keep in mind that when we claim God's conditional promises, this "if it be your will" must always be stated or implied.

Most Bibles today have cross-references listed in the side column. When reading a Bible promise, I recommend that you look up some of the cross-references to make sure you are interpreting the promise rightly.

8. When interpreting the promises of God, let the context determine the proper meaning of biblical words. I'll illustrate my point with 2 Corinthians 8:9 (NASB): "For you know the grace of our Lord Jesus Christ, that though He was rich, yet for your sake He became poor, so that you through His poverty might become rich." Some have claimed this verse as a promise of financial prosperity. Yet, this understanding of the verse does not fit the context. Notice that if Paul was intending to say that financial prosperity is provided for in the atonement, he was offering the Corinthians something that he himself did not possess at the time. Indeed, in 1 Corinthians 4:11 (NASB) Paul informed these same individuals that he was "hungry and thirsty," "poorly clothed," and "homeless." Contextually, it seems clear that 2 Corinthians 8:9 is speaking about *spiritual* prosperity, not financial prosperity. This fits both the immediate context in 2 Corinthians and the broader context of Paul's other writings.

Another illustration might be found in Isaiah 53:5: "He was pierced for our transgressions, he was crushed for our iniquities...by his wounds we are healed." Some have claimed this verse as a promise of physical healing, but spiritual healing of the sin problem seems to be in view. The Hebrew word for healing *(napha)* can refer not only to physical healing but also to spiritual healing. The context of Isaiah 53:4-5 points to spiritual healing. After all, "transgressions" and "iniquities" set the context for what is "healed." Further, numerous verses in Scripture substantiate the view that physical healing in mortal life is not guaranteed in the atonement and that it is not always God's will to heal. The apostle Paul couldn't heal Timothy's stomach problem (1 Timothy 5:23) nor could he heal Trophimus at Miletus (2 Timothy 4:20) or Epaphroditus (Philippians 2:25-27). Paul spoke of "a bodily illness" he had (Galatians 4:13-15 NASB). He also suffered a "thorn in the flesh" which God allowed him to retain (2 Corinthians 12:7-9). God certainly allowed Job to go through a time of physical suffering (Job 1–2). In none of these cases did these individuals act as if they thought their healing was promised in the atonement. They accepted their situations and trusted in God's grace for sustenance.

Here is a review of the principles we have discussed:

Principles for Interpreting Bible Promises

1. Promises made to *specific* individuals are not intended to be promises for *all* believers.

2. Promises made to Old Testament Israelites are generally not promises to people today.

3. *Some* Bible promises made in the Old Testament *are* applicable to today. These would include promises based on God's nature, promises with New Testament parallels, and general promises to "those who trust in the Lord."

4. "Wisdom sayings" in the book of Proverbs are not intended to be Bible promises.

5. Words uttered by human beings that are recorded in Scripture are not necessarily Bible promises.

6. Some Bible promises are unconditional, whereas others are conditional.

7. When interpreting the promises of God, always keep in mind what other Scriptures on the same subject reveal.

8. When interpreting the promises of God, let the context determine the proper meaning of biblical words.

When Life Throws You a Punch...

The fact that God has given us many wonderful promises in the Bible is not a guarantee that our lives will be without pain or difficult circumstances. Among the biblical saints who suffered are Job (Job 1–2), the apostle Paul (2 Corinthians 12:9), Timothy (1 Timothy 5:23), Epaphroditus (Philippians 2:25-27), and Trophimus (2 Timothy 4:20). Christians who believe in the promises of God will still get sick, will go through trials and tribulations, and may even encounter tragedy. As we read in the book of Job, "Man is born to trouble as surely as sparks fly upward" (Job 5:7), and "Man born of woman is of few days and full of trouble" (Job 14:1).

But the good news is that we are never alone in troublesome situations. The God of promises is always there to see us through (Psalm 46:1; 50:15). And, very often, it is the very promises of God that enable us to patiently endure through our difficult circumstances (2 Peter 1:4).

Having said that, I now invite you to drink richly from the promises of God in the following pages. May the Lord encourage you and bless you through these promises!

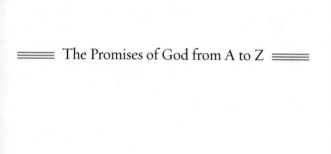

The Promises of God from A to Z

A

=== Abiding in Christ ===

Obey Christ, and you will experience joy

If you obey my commands, you will remain in my love, just as I have obeyed my Father's commands and remain in his love. I have told you this so that my joy may be in you and that your joy may be complete.

—JOHN 15:10-11

Abiding in Christ yields fruit

If a man remains in me and I in him, he will bear much fruit; apart from me you can do nothing.

— JOHN 15:5

God's love is made complete in the one who abides

If anyone obeys his word, God's love is truly made complete in him. This is how we know we are in him: Whoever claims to live in him must walk as Jesus did.

—1 JOHN 2:5-6

Acceptance

Christ will never reject any who come to Him

All that the Father gives me will come to me, and whoever comes to me I will never drive away.

—JOHN 6:37

God will draw near to those who draw near to Him

Come near to God and he will come near to you.

—JAMES 4:8

God provides absolute proof of His love for us

God demonstrates his own love for us in this: While we were still sinners, Christ died for us.

—ROMANS 5:8

God cleanses the stain of sin from your soul

"Come now, let us reason together," says the Lord. "Though your sins are like scarlet, they shall be as white as snow; though they are red as crimson, they shall be like wool."

—ISAIAH 1:18

We are brought near through Christ

In Christ Jesus you who once were far away have been brought near through the blood of Christ.

—EPHESIANS 2:13

We are recipients of salvation, not wrath

God did not appoint us to suffer wrath but to receive salvation through our Lord Jesus Christ.

—1 THESSALONIANS 5:9

Those who trust in Jesus are saved from wrath

Since we have now been justified by his blood, how much more shall we be saved from God's wrath through him!

—ROMANS 5:9

God completely removes sin from His children

As far as the east is from the west, so far has he removed our transgressions from us.

—PSALM 103:12

Adoption

Those who believe in Jesus are God's children

To all who received him, to those who believed in his name, he gave the right to become children of God.

—JOHN 1:12

You are all sons of God through faith in Christ Jesus.

—GALATIANS 3:26

We are members of God's household

You are no longer foreigners and aliens, but fellow citizens with God's people and members of God's household.

— EPHESIANS 2:19

Because of God's love, we are His children

How great is the love the Father has lavished on us, that we should be called children of God! And that is what we are!

— 1 JOHN 3:1

We are not slaves but God's children with an inheritance

Because you are sons, God sent the Spirit of his Son into our hearts, the Spirit who calls out, "Abba, Father." So you are no longer a slave, but a son; and since you are a son, God has made you also an heir.

— GALATIANS 4:6-7

We are not slaves to fear but God's children

Those who are led by the Spirit of God are sons of God. For you did not receive a spirit that makes you a slave again to fear, but you received the Spirit of sonship. And by him we cry, "Abba, Father."

— ROMANS 8:14-15

God's children are conformed to the likeness of Jesus

Those God foreknew he also predestined to be conformed to

the likeness of his Son, that he might be the firstborn among many brothers.

—ROMANS 8:29

God will lovingly discipline His children

The Lord disciplines those he loves, and he punishes everyone he accepts as a son. Endure hardship as discipline; God is treating you as sons.

—HEBREWS 12:6-7

Aging and Dying

God is our guide to the very end of our lives

This God is our God for ever and ever; he will be our guide even to the end.

—PSALM 48:14

Our bodies may age, but our spirits are renewed

We do not lose heart. Though outwardly we are wasting away, yet inwardly we are being renewed day by day.

—2 CORINTHIANS 4:16

God will abolish death

He will swallow up death forever. The Sovereign Lord will wipe away the tears from all faces.

—ISAIAH 25:8

Death will be swallowed up in victory

When the perishable has been clothed with the imperishable, and the mortal with immortality, then the saying that is written will come true: "Death has been swallowed up in victory."

—1 CORINTHIANS 15:54

Permanent resurrection bodies await us

We know that if the earthly tent we live in is destroyed, we have a building from God, an eternal house in heaven, not built by human hands.

—2 CORINTHIANS 5:1

Anger

Unrighteous anger brings judgment

I tell you that anyone who is angry with his brother will be subject to judgment. Again, anyone who says to his brother, "Raca," is answerable to the Sanhedrin. But anyone who says, "You fool!" will be in danger of the fire of hell.

—MATTHEW 5:22

God will avenge us

Do not take revenge, my friends, but leave room for God's wrath, for it is written: "It is mine to avenge; I will repay," says the Lord.

—ROMANS 12:19 (SEE ALSO HEBREWS 10:30)

God's anger is short-lived

His anger lasts only a moment, but his favor lasts a lifetime; weeping may remain for a night, but rejoicing comes in the morning.

—PSALM 30:5

Anxiety

The Lord sustains us in our troubles

Cast your cares on the Lord and he will sustain you; he will never let the righteous fall.

—PSALM 55:22

God is the source of perfect peace

Do not be anxious about anything, but in everything, by prayer and petition, with thanksgiving, present your requests to God. And the peace of God, which transcends all understanding, will guard your hearts and your minds in Christ Jesus.

—PHILIPPIANS 4:6-7

Christ gives us peace

Peace I leave with you; my peace I give you. I do not give to you as the world gives. Do not let your hearts be troubled and do not be afraid.

—JOHN 14:27

I have told you these things, so that in me you may have peace. In this world you will have trouble. But take heart! I have overcome the world.

—JOHN 16:33

Christ gives us rest
Come to me, all you who are weary and burdened, and I will give you rest.

—MATTHEW 11:28

Even in our troubles, God works for our good
We know that in all things God works for the good of those who love him, who have been called according to his purpose.

—ROMANS 8:28

Assurance of Salvation

God's people will never perish
My sheep listen to my voice; I know them, and they follow me. I give them eternal life, and they shall never perish; no one can snatch them out of my hand. My Father, who has given them to me, is greater than all; no one can snatch them out of my Father's hand.

—JOHN 10:27-29

God's people are sealed by the Holy Spirit

Having believed, you were marked in him with a seal, the promised Holy Spirit, who is a deposit guaranteeing our inheritance until the redemption of those who are God's possession.

—EPHESIANS 1:13-14 (SEE ALSO EPHESIANS 4:30)

Atonement

We are redeemed and forgiven

In him we have redemption through his blood, the forgiveness of sins, in accordance with the riches of God's grace.

—EPHESIANS 1:7

We are forgiven

He forgave us all our sins, having canceled the written code, with its regulations, that was against us and that stood opposed to us; he took it away, nailing it to the cross.

—COLOSSIANS 2:13-14

We are saved from God's wrath

Since we have now been justified by his blood, how much more shall we be saved from God's wrath through him!

—ROMANS 5:9

Jesus died for the sins of the world

He is the atoning sacrifice for our sins, and not only for ours but also for the sins of the whole world.

—1 JOHN 2:2

Jesus' sacrifice takes away our sins

Christ was sacrificed once to take away the sins of many people; and he will appear a second time, not to bear sin, but to bring salvation to those who are waiting for him.

—HEBREWS 9:28

B

Backsliding

God can deliver you from any temptation
No temptation has seized you except what is common to man. And God is faithful; he will not let you be tempted beyond what you can bear. But when you are tempted, he will also provide a way out so that you can stand up under it.

—1 Corinthians 10:13

Dependence on the Holy Spirit brings victory
Live by the Spirit, and you will not gratify the desires of the sinful nature.

—Galatians 5:16

Those who believe in Jesus overcome the world
Everyone born of God overcomes the world. This is the victory that has overcome the world, even our faith. Who is it that overcomes the world? Only he who believes that Jesus is the Son of God.

—1 John 5:4-5

God forgives and cleanses us if we confess
If we confess our sins, he is faithful and just and will forgive us our sins and purify us from all unrighteousness.

—1 JOHN 1:9

God gives the crown of life to those who persevere
Blessed is the man who perseveres under trial, because when he has stood the test, he will receive the crown of life that God has promised to those who love him.

—JAMES 1:12

Belief

Faith in God brings big results
Everything is possible for him who believes.

—MARK 9:23

Those who believe in Jesus receive eternal life
For God so loved the world that he gave his one and only Son, that whoever believes in him shall not perish but have eternal life.

—JOHN 3:16 (SEE ALSO ACTS 10:43; 16:31)

Whoever believes in the Son has eternal life, but whoever rejects the Son will not see life, for God's wrath remains on him.

—JOHN 3:36 (SEE ALSO JOHN 3:18; 6:47)

Those who believe in Jesus are spiritually satisfied
Jesus declared, "I am the bread of life. He who comes to me will never go hungry, and he who believes in me will never be thirsty."

—JOHN 6:35

Those who believe in Jesus will not remain in darkness
I have come into the world as a light, so that no one who believes in me should stay in darkness.

—JOHN 12:46

Those who believe in Jesus will be resurrected
Jesus said to her, "I am the resurrection and the life. He who believes in me will live, even though he dies; and whoever lives and believes in me will never die."

—JOHN 11:25-26

Benevolence

God gives you all you need to do good
God is able to make all grace abound to you, so that in all things at all times, having all that you need, you will abound in every good work.

—2 CORINTHIANS 9:8

God will not forget your good work

God is not unjust; he will not forget your work and the love you have shown him as you have helped his people and continue to help them.

—HEBREWS 6:10

Give secretly, and God will reward you

When you give to the needy, do not let your left hand know what your right hand is doing, so that your giving may be in secret. Then your Father, who sees what is done in secret, will reward you.

—MATTHEW 6:3-4

Doing good to others is doing good to Christ

I tell you the truth, whatever you did for one of the least of these brothers of mine, you did for me.

—MATTHEW 25:40

God blesses those who help the weak

Blessed is he who has regard for the weak; the Lord delivers him in times of trouble. The Lord will protect him and preserve his life.

—PSALM 41:1-2

Bereavement

The death of Christians is precious to God

Precious in the sight of the Lord is the death of his saints.

—PSALM 116:15

God comforts those who mourn

Blessed are those who mourn, for they will be comforted.

—MATTHEW 5:4

God will abolish tears and death

He will wipe every tear from their eyes. There will be no more death or mourning or crying or pain, for the old order of things has passed away.

—REVELATION 21:4

A wonderful destiny awaits those who love God

No eye has seen, no ear has heard, no mind has conceived what God has prepared for those who love him.

—1 CORINTHIANS 2:9

Permanent resurrection bodies await us

We know that if the earthly tent we live in is destroyed, we have a building from God, an eternal house in heaven, not built by human hands.

—2 CORINTHIANS 5:1

45

We will be resurrected

I am the resurrection and the life. He who believes in me will live, even though he dies.

—JOHN 11:25

Bible

God's Word endures forever

Heaven and earth will pass away, but my words will never pass away.

—MARK 13:31

God's Word is powerfully effective

It will not return to me empty, but will accomplish what I desire and achieve the purpose for which I sent it.

—ISAIAH 55:11

Scripture is inspired and equips us

All Scripture is God-breathed and is useful for teaching, rebuking, correcting and training in righteousness, so that the man of God may be thoroughly equipped for every good work.

—2 TIMOTHY 3:16-17

God's Word revives the soul

The law of the Lord is perfect, reviving the soul. The statutes of the Lord are trustworthy, making wise the simple. The precepts of the Lord are right, giving joy to the heart. The commands of the Lord are radiant, giving light to the eyes.

—PSALM 19:7-8

Tampering with God's Word brings judgment

I warn everyone who hears the words of the prophecy of this book: If anyone adds anything to them, God will add to him the plagues described in this book. And if anyone takes words away from this book of prophecy, God will take away from him his share in the tree of life and in the holy city, which are described in this book.

—REVELATION 22:18-19

Blessing

Those who trust the Lord are blessed

Blessed is the man who trusts in the Lord, whose confidence is in him.

—JEREMIAH 17:7

Those who fear the Lord are blessed

Blessed are all who fear the Lord, who walk in his ways.

—PSALM 128:1

The poor in spirit are blessed

Blessed are the poor in spirit, for theirs is the kingdom of heaven.

—Matthew 5:3

Those who mourn are blessed

Blessed are those who mourn, for they will be comforted.

—Matthew 5:4

The meek are blessed

Blessed are the meek, for they will inherit the earth.

—Matthew 5:5

Those who yearn for righteousness are blessed

Blessed are those who hunger and thirst for righteousness, for they will be filled.

—Matthew 5:6

The merciful are blessed

Blessed are the merciful, for they will be shown mercy.

—Matthew 5:7

The pure in heart are blessed

Blessed are the pure in heart, for they will see God.

—Matthew 5:8

The peacemakers are blessed

Blessed are the peacemakers, for they will be called sons of God.

—Matthew 5:9

Those persecuted because of righteousness are blessed

Blessed are those who are persecuted because of righteousness, for theirs is the kingdom of heaven.

—Matthew 5:10

Blessed are you when people insult you, persecute you and falsely say all kinds of evil against you because of me. Rejoice and be glad, because great is your reward in heaven.

—Matthew 5:11-12

Blood of Jesus

We are redeemed and forgiven

In him we have redemption through his blood, the forgiveness of sins, in accordance with the riches of God's grace.

—Ephesians 1:7

We are redeemed

It was not with perishable things such as silver or gold that you were redeemed from the empty way of life handed down to you from your forefathers, but with the precious blood of Christ, a lamb without blemish or defect.

—I PETER 1:18-19

We are purified from all sin

If we walk in the light, as he is in the light, we have fellowship with one another, and the blood of Jesus, his Son, purifies us from all sin.

—I JOHN 1:7

Our consciences are cleansed

How much more, then, will the blood of Christ, who through the eternal Spirit offered himself unblemished to God, cleanse our consciences from acts that lead to death, so that we may serve the living God!

—HEBREWS 9:14

============ Boldness ============

God is always faithful to us

Let us hold unswervingly to the hope we profess, for he who promised is faithful.

—HEBREWS 10:23

God is always for us

If God is for us, who can be against us? He who did not spare his own Son, but gave him up for us all—how will he not also, along with him, graciously give us all things?

—ROMANS 8:31-32

We can be confident in approaching God
This is the confidence we have in approaching God: that if we ask anything according to his will, he hears us. And if we know that he hears us—whatever we ask—we know that we have what we asked of him.

—1 JOHN 5:14-15

We are conquerors in Christ
In all these things we are more than conquerors through him who loved us.

—ROMANS 8:37

Those who trust in Jesus are empowered
I tell you the truth, anyone who has faith in me will do what I have been doing. He will do even greater things than these, because I am going to the Father.

—JOHN 14:12

Burdens

The Lord sustains us in our troubles
Cast your cares on the Lord and he will sustain you; he will never let the righteous fall.

—PSALM 55:22

Christ gives us rest

Come to me, all you who are weary and burdened, and I will give you rest.

—MATTHEW 11:28

Turning anxieties over to God yields perfect peace

Do not be anxious about anything, but in everything, by prayer and petition, with thanksgiving, present your requests to God. And the peace of God, which transcends all understanding, will guard your hearts and your minds in Christ Jesus.

—PHILIPPIANS 4:6-7

God is our refuge and strength

God is our refuge and strength, an ever-present help in trouble.

—PSALM 46:1

C

God cares for us and will meet all our needs

My God will meet all your needs according to his glorious riches in Christ Jesus.

—PHILIPPIANS 4:19

God will take care of our earthly needs

Do not worry about your life, what you will eat or drink; or about your body, what you will wear. Is not life more important than food, and the body more important than clothes? Look at the birds of the air; they do not sow or reap or store away in barns, and yet your heavenly Father feeds them. Are you not much more valuable than they?

—MATTHEW 6:25-26

The Lord will take care of us in our troubles

Cast your cares on the Lord and he will sustain you; he will never let the righteous fall.

—PSALM 55:22

Carnality

The Holy Spirit empowers us to overcome sinful desires

Live by the Spirit, and you will not gratify the desires of the sinful nature.

—GALATIANS 5:16

Pleasing the Holy Spirit yields eternal life

The one who sows to please his sinful nature, from that nature will reap destruction; the one who sows to please the Spirit, from the Spirit will reap eternal life.

—GALATIANS 6:8

The mind controlled by the Spirit is life and peace

Those who live according to the sinful nature have their minds set on what that nature desires; but those who live in accordance with the Spirit have their minds set on what the Spirit desires. The mind of sinful man is death, but the mind controlled by the Spirit is life and peace.

—ROMANS 8:5-6

Character

God abundantly blesses a righteous character

The Lord God is a sun and shield; the Lord bestows favor

and honor; no good thing does he withhold from those whose walk is blameless.

—PSALM 84:11

Those who yearn for righteousness will be satisfied

Blessed are those who hunger and thirst for righteousness, for they will be filled.

—MATTHEW 5:6

Righteousness yields peace and confidence

The fruit of righteousness will be peace; the effect of righteousness will be quietness and confidence forever.

—ISAIAH 32:17

Charity

God will bless you if you bless others

Give, and it will be given to you. A good measure, pressed down, shaken together and running over, will be poured into your lap. For with the measure you use, it will be measured to you.

—LUKE 6:38

Give secretly, and God will bless you

When you give to the needy, do not let your left hand know what your right hand is doing, so that your giving may be in secret. Then your Father, who sees what is done in secret, will reward you.

—MATTHEW 6:3-4

God will reward us for charity to the disenfranchised

When you give a banquet, invite the poor, the crippled, the lame, the blind, and you will be blessed. Although they cannot repay you, you will be repaid at the resurrection of the righteous.

—LUKE 14:13-14

Charitable kindness to children brings blessing

If anyone gives even a cup of cold water to one of these little ones because he is my disciple, I tell you the truth, he will certainly not lose his reward.

—MATTHEW 10:42

God blesses those who help the weak

Blessed is he who has regard for the weak; the Lord delivers him in times of trouble. The Lord will protect him and preserve his life.

—PSALM 41:1-2

Charity to others is charity to Christ

I tell you the truth, whatever you did for one of the least of these brothers of mine, you did for me.

—MATTHEW 25:40

Children

Little children are welcome in God's kingdom

Let the little children come to me, and do not hinder them, for the kingdom of heaven belongs to such as these.

—MATTHEW 19:14 (SEE ALSO MARK 10:14-16)

Everyone is offered the blessing of salvation

Repent and be baptized, every one of you, in the name of Jesus Christ for the forgiveness of your sins. And you will receive the gift of the Holy Spirit. The promise is for you and your children and for all who are far off—for all whom the Lord our God will call.

—ACTS 2:38-39

Obedience to parents yields longevity

Children, obey your parents in the Lord, for this is right. "Honor your father and mother"—which is the first commandment with a promise—"that it may go well with you and that you may enjoy long life on the earth."

—EPHESIANS 6:1-3 (SEE ALSO COLOSSIANS 3:20)

God blesses the children of righteous parents

From everlasting to everlasting the Lord's love is with those who fear him, and his righteousness with their children's children.

—PSALM 103:17

Becoming humble like a child yields greatness

Whoever humbles himself like this child is the greatest in the kingdom of heaven.

—MATTHEW 18:4

Children of God

Those who believe in Jesus are God's children

To all who received him, to those who believed in his name, he gave the right to become children of God.

—JOHN 1:12

We become God's children through faith in Jesus

You are all sons of God through faith in Christ Jesus.

—GALATIANS 3:26

God's children are not slaves to fear

Those who are led by the Spirit of God are sons of God. For you did not receive a spirit that makes you a slave again to fear, but you received the Spirit of sonship. And by him we cry, "Abba, Father."

—ROMANS 8:14-15 (SEE ALSO GALATIANS 4:6-7)

As God's children, we are heirs of God

The Spirit himself testifies with our spirit that we are God's children. Now if we are children, then we are heirs—heirs of

God and co-heirs with Christ, if indeed we share in his sufferings in order that we may also share in his glory.

—ROMANS 8:16-17

As children of God, our future is glorious

Dear friends, now we are children of God, and what we will be has not yet been made known. But we know that when he appears, we shall be like him, for we shall see him as he is.

—1 JOHN 3:2

Christ's Return

Jesus will come again physically and visibly

This same Jesus, who has been taken from you into heaven, will come back in the same way you have seen him go into heaven.

—ACTS 1:11

Every eye will witness the Second Coming

Look, he is coming with the clouds, and every eye will see him, even those who pierced him; and all the peoples of the earth will mourn because of him.

—REVELATION 1:7

Christ will come at an hour we do not expect

You also must be ready, because the Son of Man will come at an hour when you do not expect him.

—LUKE 12:40

The gospel will be preached to all nations before the Second Coming

This gospel of the kingdom will be preached in the whole world as a testimony to all nations, and then the end will come.

—MATTHEW 24:14

When Christ comes, we will receive resurrection bodies

Our citizenship is in heaven. And we eagerly await a Savior from there, the Lord Jesus Christ, who, by the power that enables him to bring everything under his control, will transform our lowly bodies so that they will be like his glorious body.

—PHILIPPIANS 3:20-21

Christ will bring ultimate and final salvation when He returns

Christ was sacrificed once to take away the sins of many people; and he will appear a second time, not to bear sin, but to bring salvation to those who are waiting for him.

—HEBREWS 9:28

Christ will come in judgment at the Second Coming
Behold, I am coming soon! My reward is with me, and I will give to everyone according to what he has done.

—REVELATION 22:12

Closeness to God

God will draw near to those who draw near to Him
Come near to God and he will come near to you.

—JAMES 4:8

The Lord is near to all who call on Him
The Lord is near to all who call on him, to all who call on him in truth.

—PSALM 145:18

We find God when we seek Him with all our heart
You will seek me and find me when you seek me with all your heart.

—JEREMIAH 29:13

We are brought near to God through the blood of Jesus
In Christ Jesus you who once were far away have been brought near through the blood of Christ.

—EPHESIANS 2:13

The pure in heart will see God

Blessed are the pure in heart, for they will see God.

—MATTHEW 5:8

Christ fellowships with the one who invites Him

Here I am! I stand at the door and knock. If anyone hears my voice and opens the door, I will come in and eat with him, and he with me.

—REVELATION 3:20

 Comfort

The Lord is close to the brokenhearted

The Lord is close to the brokenhearted and saves those who are crushed in spirit.

—PSALM 34:18

God will wipe away every tear

The Lamb at the center of the throne will be their shepherd; he will lead them to springs of living water. And God will wipe away every tear from their eyes.

—REVELATION 7:17

The Lord will sustain us

Cast your cares on the Lord and he will sustain you; he will never let the righteous fall.

—PSALM 55:22

Christ gives us rest

Come to me, all you who are weary and burdened, and I will give you rest.

—MATTHEW 11:28

The Lord is our refuge

The Lord is good, a refuge in times of trouble. He cares for those who trust in him.

—NAHUM 1:7

God comforts us

Praise be to the God and Father of our Lord Jesus Christ, the Father of compassion and the God of all comfort, who comforts us in all our troubles, so that we can comfort those in any trouble with the comfort we ourselves have received from God. For just as the sufferings of Christ flow over into our lives, so also through Christ our comfort overflows.

—2 CORINTHIANS 1:3-5

Christ is always with us

Surely I am with you always, to the very end of the age.

—MATTHEW 28:20

Companionship with God

Christ fellowships with those who invite Him

Here I am! I stand at the door and knock. If anyone hears my voice and opens the door, I will come in and eat with him, and he with me.

— REVELATION 3:20

The Lord is near to those who call on Him

The Lord is near to all who call on him, to all who call on him in truth.

— PSALM 145:18

We have fellowship with God when we walk in the light

If we walk in the light, as he is in the light, we have fellowship with one another, and the blood of Jesus, his Son, purifies us from all sin.

— 1 JOHN 1:7

God draws near to those who draw near to Him

Come near to God and he will come near to you.

— JAMES 4:8

We find God when we seek Him with all our hearts

You will seek me and find me when you seek me with all your heart.

— JEREMIAH 29:13

The Lord is full of compassion
The Lord is full of compassion and mercy.

—JAMES 5:11

The Lord is compassionate to all
The Lord is good to all; he has compassion on all he has made.

—PSALM 145:9

God's compassion is like a loving parent's
As a father has compassion on his children, so the Lord has compassion on those who fear him.

—PSALM 103:13

The Lord's compassions never fail
Because of the Lord's great love we are not consumed, for his compassions never fail. They are new every morning.

—LAMENTATIONS 3:22-23

The Lord desires to show compassion
The Lord longs to be gracious to you; he rises to show you compassion. For the Lord is a God of justice. Blessed are all who wait for him!

—ISAIAH 30:18

Condemnation

There is no condemnation for those in Christ
There is now no condemnation for those who are in Christ Jesus.

—ROMANS 8:1

We are new creatures in Christ
If anyone is in Christ, he is a new creation; the old has gone, the new has come!

—2 CORINTHIANS 5:17

God seeks to save us, not condemn us
God did not send his Son into the world to condemn the world, but to save the world through him. Whoever believes in him is not condemned, but whoever does not believe stands condemned already because he has not believed in the name of God's one and only Son.

—JOHN 3:17-18

Trusting in Jesus rescues one from condemnation
Whoever hears my word and believes him who sent me has eternal life and will not be condemned; he has crossed over from death to life.

—JOHN 5:24

God has completely removed our transgressions

As far as the east is from the west, so far has he removed our transgressions from us.

—PSALM 103:12

God will no longer remember our sins

I will forgive their wickedness and will remember their sins no more.

—HEBREWS 8:12

God blots out our transgressions

I, even I, am he who blots out your transgressions, for my own sake, and remembers your sins no more.

—ISAIAH 43:25

Confession

God cleanses us of all sins when we confess

If we confess our sins, he is faithful and just and will forgive us our sins and purify us from all unrighteousness.

—1 JOHN 1:9

Confession to each other brings healing

Confess your sins to each other and pray for each other so

67

that you may be healed. The prayer of a righteous man is powerful and effective.

—JAMES 5:16

Our confession of Jesus brings salvation

If you confess with your mouth, "Jesus is Lord," and believe in your heart that God raised him from the dead, you will be saved.

—ROMANS 10:9

Christ will acknowledge us if we acknowledge Him

Whoever acknowledges me before men, I will also acknowledge him before my Father in heaven.

—MATTHEW 10:32 (SEE ALSO LUKE 12:8)

Confidence

We can do everything through Christ

I can do everything through him who gives me strength.

—PHILIPPIANS 4:13

We are conquerors in Christ

In all these things we are more than conquerors through him who loved us.

—ROMANS 8:37

We can be confident in approaching God

This is the confidence we have in approaching God: that if we ask anything according to his will, he hears us. And if we know that he hears us—whatever we ask—we know that we have what we asked of him.

—1 JOHN 5:14-15

Our confidence will be richly rewarded

Do not throw away your confidence; it will be richly rewarded. You need to persevere so that when you have done the will of God, you will receive what he has promised.

—HEBREWS 10:35-36

We should be unswerving, for God is faithful

Let us hold unswervingly to the hope we profess, for he who promised is faithful.

—HEBREWS 10:23

Conflict

Peacemakers are sons of God

Blessed are the peacemakers, for they will be called sons of God.

—MATTHEW 5:9

The God of peace is with us

Aim for perfection, listen to my appeal, be of one mind, live in peace. And the God of love and peace will be with you.

— 2 CORINTHIANS 13:11

Whatever you have learned or received or heard from me, or seen in me—put it into practice. And the God of peace will be with you.

— PHILIPPIANS 4:9

Christ gives us peace

Peace I leave with you; my peace I give you. I do not give to you as the world gives. Do not let your hearts be troubled and do not be afraid.

— JOHN 14:27

Confusion

Christ's followers will not walk in darkness

I am the light of the world. Whoever follows me will never walk in darkness, but will have the light of life.

— JOHN 8:12

God gives us wisdom

If any of you lacks wisdom, he should ask God, who gives generously to all without finding fault, and it will be given to him.

— JAMES 1:5

God guides us

I will instruct you and teach you in the way you should go; I will counsel you and watch over you.

— PSALM 32:8

The Lord makes our steps firm

If the Lord delights in a man's way, he makes his steps firm; though he stumble, he will not fall, for the Lord upholds him with his hand.

— PSALM 37:23-24

God gives us a spirit of power

God did not give us a spirit of timidity, but a spirit of power, of love and of self-discipline.

— 2 TIMOTHY 1:7

============ Consolation ============

The Lord is close to the brokenhearted

The righteous cry out, and the Lord hears them; he delivers them from all their troubles. The Lord is close to the brokenhearted and saves those who are crushed in spirit.

— PSALM 34:17-18

The Lord heals the brokenhearted

He heals the brokenhearted and binds up their wounds.

— PSALM 147:3

Christ gives us rest

Come to me, all you who are weary and burdened, and I will give you rest.

—MATTHEW 11:28

The Lord sustains us

Cast your cares on the Lord and he will sustain you.

—PSALM 55:22

The Lord is our refuge

The Lord is good, a refuge in times of trouble. He cares for those who trust in him.

—NAHUM 1:7

Contentment

The mind focused on God has perfect peace

You will keep in perfect peace him whose mind is steadfast, because he trusts in you.

—ISAIAH 26:3

The mind controlled by the Spirit has peace

The mind of sinful man is death, but the mind controlled by the Spirit is life and peace.

—ROMANS 8:6

Turning our anxieties over to God yields perfect peace

Do not be anxious about anything, but in everything, by prayer and petition, with thanksgiving, present your requests to God. And the peace of God, which transcends all understanding, will guard your hearts and your minds in Christ Jesus.

—PHILIPPIANS 4:6-7

Be content, for God will provide

Do not worry, saying, "What shall we eat?" or "What shall we drink?" or "What shall we wear?" For the pagans run after all these things, and your heavenly Father knows that you need them. But seek first his kingdom and his righteousness, and all these things will be given to you as well.

—MATTHEW 6:31-33

Be content, for God will never forsake you

Keep your lives free from the love of money and be content with what you have, because God has said, "Never will I leave you; never will I forsake you."

—HEBREWS 13:5

Be content, for God is in control

We know that in all things God works for the good of those who love him, who have been called according to his purpose.

—ROMANS 8:28

Courage

We can do all things through Christ

I can do everything through him who gives me strength.

— PHILIPPIANS 4:13

God is completely for us

If God is for us, who can be against us? He who did not spare his own Son, but gave him up for us all—how will he not also, along with him, graciously give us all things?

— ROMANS 8:31-32

God upholds us

Do not fear, for I am with you; do not be dismayed, for I am your God. I will strengthen you and help you; I will uphold you with my righteous right hand.

— ISAIAH 41:10

D

Those who follow Jesus never permanently die
I tell you the truth, if anyone keeps my word, he will never
see death.

—JOHN 8:51

God will abolish death
He will swallow up death forever. The Sovereign Lord will
wipe away the tears from all faces.

—ISAIAH 25:8

Death will be swallowed up in victory
When the perishable has been clothed with the imperishable, and the mortal with immortality, then the saying that
is written will come true: "Death has been swallowed up in
victory."

—1 CORINTHIANS 15:54

Death cannot separate us from Christ
I am convinced that neither death nor life, neither angels nor

demons, neither the present nor the future, nor any powers, neither height nor depth, nor anything else in all creation, will be able to separate us from the love of God that is in Christ Jesus our Lord.

—ROMANS 8:38-39

Permanent resurrection bodies await us

We know that if the earthly tent we live in is destroyed, we have a building from God, an eternal house in heaven, not built by human hands.

—2 CORINTHIANS 5:1

God is our guide to the very end of our lives

This God is our God for ever and ever; he will be our guide even to the end.

—PSALM 48:14

Decisions

God gives wisdom to those who ask in faith

If any of you lacks wisdom, he should ask God, who gives generously to all without finding fault, and it will be given to him.

—JAMES 1:5

God will guide us

I will instruct you and teach you in the way you should go; I will counsel you and watch over you.

— PSALM 32:8

The Holy Spirit will help and guide us

I will ask the Father, and he will give you another Counselor to be with you forever—the Spirit of truth.

— JOHN 14:16-17

Minds transformed by God and His Word can discern His will

Do not conform any longer to the pattern of this world, but be transformed by the renewing of your mind. Then you will be able to test and approve what God's will is—his good, pleasing and perfect will.

— ROMANS 12:2

Dejection

God draws near to those who draw near to Him

Come near to God and he will come near to you.

— JAMES 4:8

Christ sympathizes with our weaknesses

We do not have a high priest who is unable to sympathize

with our weaknesses, but we have one who has been tempted in every way, just as we are—yet was without sin.

—HEBREWS 4:15

The Lord's compassions never fail

Because of the Lord's great love we are not consumed, for his compassions never fail. They are new every morning.

—LAMENTATIONS 3:22-23

God's love is everlasting

From everlasting to everlasting the Lord's love is with those who fear him.

—PSALM 103:17

God provides absolute proof of His love

God demonstrates his own love for us in this: While we were still sinners, Christ died for us.

—ROMANS 5:8

Deliverance

God guards Christians who fear Him

The angel of the Lord encamps around those who fear him, and he delivers them.

—PSALM 34:7

The Lord delivers the righteous from trouble

The righteous cry out, and the Lord hears them; he delivers them from all their troubles.

—PSALM 34:17

The Lord rescues godly people

The Lord knows how to rescue godly men from trials.

—2 PETER 2:9

God delivers us from our troubles

Call upon me in the day of trouble; I will deliver you, and you will honor me.

—PSALM 50:15

The truth sets us free

You will know the truth, and the truth will set you free.

—JOHN 8:32

Jesus sets us free

If the Son sets you free, you will be free indeed.

—JOHN 8:36

The Lord delivers us from Satan

The Lord is faithful, and he will strengthen and protect you from the evil one.

—2 THESSALONIANS 3:3

God delivers us from temptations

No temptation has seized you except what is common to man. And God is faithful; he will not let you be tempted beyond what you can bear. But when you are tempted, he will also provide a way out so that you can stand up under it.

—1 CORINTHIANS 10:13

Jesus helps us during temptations

Because he himself suffered when he was tempted, he is able to help those who are being tempted.

—HEBREWS 2:18

Depression

God heals the brokenhearted

He heals the brokenhearted and binds up their wounds.

—PSALM 147:3

God comforts those who mourn

Blessed are those who mourn, for they will be comforted.

—MATTHEW 5:4

Turning our anxieties over to God yields perfect peace

Do not be anxious about anything, but in everything, by

prayer and petition, with thanksgiving, present your requests to God. And the peace of God, which transcends all understanding, will guard your hearts and your minds in Christ Jesus.

—PHILIPPIANS 4:6-7

God will deliver us from our troubles

Call upon me in the day of trouble; I will deliver you, and you will honor me.

—PSALM 50:15

The Lord will sustain us in our troubles

Cast your cares on the Lord and he will sustain you.

—PSALM 55:22

God empowers those who hope in Him

Those who hope in the Lord will renew their strength. They will soar on wings like eagles; they will run and not grow weary, they will walk and not be faint.

—ISAIAH 40:31

Suffering produces perseverance

We also rejoice in our sufferings, because we know that suffering produces perseverance.

—ROMANS 5:3

Desertion

The Lord will never reject His people
The Lord will not reject his people; he will never forsake his inheritance.

—PSALM 94:14

The Lord will never forsake us
Never will I leave you; never will I forsake you.

—HEBREWS 13:5

The Lord will not forsake the faithful
The Lord loves the just and will not forsake his faithful ones. They will be protected forever, but the offspring of the wicked will be cut off.

—PSALM 37:28

Christ is with us always
Surely I am with you always, to the very end of the age.

—MATTHEW 28:20

Even when we are faithless, God remains faithful
If we are faithless, he will remain faithful, for he cannot disown himself.

—2 TIMOTHY 2:13

Despair

God gives us strength
He gives strength to the weary and increases the power of the weak.

—ISAIAH 40:29

God is our refuge
God is our refuge and strength, an ever-present help in trouble.

—PSALM 46:1

Christ provides relief
Come to me, all you who are weary and burdened, and I will give you rest.

—MATTHEW 11:28

Our troubles fade in comparison to our future glory
We do not lose heart. Though outwardly we are wasting away, yet inwardly we are being renewed day by day. For our light and momentary troubles are achieving for us an eternal glory that far outweighs them all. So we fix our eyes not on what is seen, but on what is unseen. For what is seen is temporary, but what is unseen is eternal.

—2 CORINTHIANS 4:16-18

Our perseverance in trials will yield the crown of life
Blessed is the man who perseveres under trial, because when

he has stood the test, he will receive the crown of life that God has promised to those who love him.

— JAMES 1:12

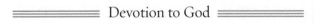

Determination

Christ is coming soon
I am coming soon. Hold on to what you have, so that no one will take your crown.

— REVELATION 3:11

We will reap a harvest if we persevere
Let us not become weary in doing good, for at the proper time we will reap a harvest if we do not give up.

— GALATIANS 6:9

Confidence will be rewarded
Do not throw away your confidence; it will be richly rewarded. You need to persevere so that when you have done the will of God, you will receive what he has promised.

— HEBREWS 10:35-36

Devotion to God

The Lord strengthens those committed to Him
The eyes of the Lord range throughout the earth to strengthen those whose hearts are fully committed to him.

— 2 CHRONICLES 16:9

The one who obeys will be blessed

The man who looks intently into the perfect law that gives freedom, and continues to do this, not forgetting what he has heard, but doing it—he will be blessed in what he does.

—JAMES 1:25

Christ answers the prayers of those devoted to Him

If you remain in me and my words remain in you, ask whatever you wish, and it will be given you.

—JOHN 15:7

God's love made complete in those who obey

We know that we have come to know him if we obey his commands. The man who says, "I know him," but does not do what he commands is a liar, and the truth is not in him. But if anyone obeys his word, God's love is truly made complete in him.

—1 JOHN 2:3-5

God loves those who obey

Whoever has my commands and obeys them, he is the one who loves me. He who loves me will be loved by my Father, and I too will love him and show myself to him.

—JOHN 14:21

Disappointment

God comforts those who mourn
Blessed are those who mourn, for they will be comforted.

—MATTHEW 5:4

The Lord is near to those who call on Him
The Lord is near to all who call on him, to all who call on him in truth.

—PSALM 145:18

Even in our troubles, God is working for our good
We know that in all things God works for the good of those who love him, who have been called according to his purpose.

—ROMANS 8:28

Discernment

God grants wisdom to those who ask in faith
If any of you lacks wisdom, he should ask God, who gives generously to all without finding fault, and it will be given to him.

—JAMES 1:5

Minds transformed by God and His Word can discern His will

Do not conform any longer to the pattern of this world, but be transformed by the renewing of your mind. Then you will be able to test and approve what God's will is—his good, pleasing and perfect will.

—ROMANS 12:2

God will guide us

I will instruct you and teach you in the way you should go; I will counsel you and watch over you.

—PSALM 32:8

Discipleship

True disciples are honored by God

Whoever serves me must follow me; and where I am, my servant also will be. My Father will honor the one who serves me.

—JOHN 12:26

Whoever loses his life for Jesus will find it

If anyone would come after me, he must deny himself and take up his cross and follow me. For whoever wants to save his life will lose it, but whoever loses his life for me will find it.

—MATTHEW 16:24-25

Disciples never walk in darkness

I am the light of the world. Whoever follows me will never walk in darkness, but will have the light of life.

—JOHN 8:12

Christ reveals Himself to obedient disciples

Whoever has my commands and obeys them, he is the one who loves me. He who loves me will be loved by my Father, and I too will love him and show myself to him.

—JOHN 14:21

We are Jesus' disciples when we obey

If you hold to my teaching, you are really my disciples.

—JOHN 8:31

Disciples bear fruit when connected to Christ

Remain in me, and I will remain in you. No branch can bear fruit by itself; it must remain in the vine. Neither can you bear fruit unless you remain in me. I am the vine; you are the branches. If a man remains in me and I in him, he will bear much fruit; apart from me you can do nothing.

—JOHN 15:4-5

Discipline

God disciplines those whom He loves

Those whom I love I rebuke and discipline. So be earnest, and repent.

— REVELATION 3:19

God lovingly disciplines us as children

The Lord disciplines those he loves, and he punishes everyone he accepts as a son. Endure hardship as discipline.

— HEBREWS 12:6-7

God disciplines us for our good

God disciplines us for our good, that we may share in his holiness. No discipline seems pleasant at the time, but painful. Later on, however, it produces a harvest of righteousness and peace for those who have been trained by it.

— HEBREWS 12:10-11

We are judged so we will not be condemned

When we are judged by the Lord, we are being disciplined so that we will not be condemned with the world.

— 1 CORINTHIANS 11:32

Scripture rebukes and corrects us
All Scripture is God-breathed and is useful for teaching, rebuking, correcting and training in righteousness.

— 2 TIMOTHY 3:16

Discouragement

Perseverance will be rewarded
Do not throw away your confidence; it will be richly rewarded. You need to persevere so that when you have done the will of God, you will receive what he has promised.

— HEBREWS 10:35-36

We will reap a harvest if we don't give up
Let us not become weary in doing good, for at the proper time we will reap a harvest if we do not give up.

— GALATIANS 6:9

Christ gives us peace
Peace I leave with you; my peace I give you. I do not give to you as the world gives. Do not let your hearts be troubled and do not be afraid.

— JOHN 14:27

The Lord renews the strength of those who hope in Him

Those who hope in the Lord will renew their strength. They will soar on wings like eagles; they will run and not grow weary, they will walk and not be faint.

—ISAIAH 40:31

Disobedience

The one who obeys God is blessed

The man who looks intently into the perfect law that gives freedom, and continues to do this, not forgetting what he has heard, but doing it—he will be blessed in what he does.

—JAMES 1:25

God's love is made complete in the one who obeys

If anyone obeys his word, God's love is truly made complete in him. This is how we know we are in him.

—1 JOHN 2:5

Obedience brings the blessing of fellowship with God

If anyone loves me, he will obey my teaching. My Father will love him, and we will come to him and make our home with him.

—JOHN 14:23

People will be held accountable for disobedience
The Son of Man is going to come in his Father's glory with his angels, and then he will reward each person according to what he has done.

— MATTHEW 16:27

Dissatisfaction

God is the true source of satisfaction
He satisfies the thirsty and fills the hungry with good things.

— PSALM 107:9

I will refresh the weary and satisfy the faint.

— JEREMIAH 31:25

Blessed are you who hunger now, for you will be satisfied.

— LUKE 6:21

Those who seek the Lord find full satisfaction in Him
The lions may grow weak and hungry, but those who seek the Lord lack no good thing.

— PSALM 34:10

God brings satisfaction to those who delight in Him
Delight yourself in the Lord and he will give you the desires of your heart.

— PSALM 37:4

Divine Protection

God guards those who fear Him
The angel of the Lord encamps around those who fear him, and he delivers them.

— PSALM 34:7

God protects the faithful
The Lord loves the just and will not forsake his faithful ones. They will be protected forever, but the offspring of the wicked will be cut off.

— PSALM 37:28

God is our great protector
He will cover you with his feathers, and under his wings you will find refuge; his faithfulness will be your shield and rampart. You will not fear the terror of night, nor the arrow that flies by day, nor the pestilence that stalks in the darkness, nor the plague that destroys at midday.

— PSALM 91:4-6

God rescues those who love Him
"Because he loves me," says the Lord, "I will rescue him; I will protect him, for he acknowledges my name."

— PSALM 91:14

God protects us from Satan
The Lord is faithful, and he will strengthen and protect you from the evil one.

— 2 THESSALONIANS 3:3

Divine Provision

Have faith, for God will care for you

If that is how God clothes the grass of the field, which is here today, and tomorrow is thrown into the fire, how much more will he clothe you, O you of little faith!

—LUKE 12:28

God will meet all needs

My God will meet all your needs according to his glorious riches in Christ Jesus.

—PHILIPPIANS 4:19

God provides for those who fear Him

He provides food for those who fear him.

—PSALM 111:5

Put God first, and temporal needs will be met

Seek first his kingdom and his righteousness, and all these things will be given to you as well.

—MATTHEW 6:33

God satisfies our hunger

He satisfies the thirsty and fills the hungry with good things.

—PSALM 107:9

Doubts of Salvation

God's people are sealed by the Holy Spirit

Having believed, you were marked in him with a seal, the promised Holy Spirit, who is a deposit guaranteeing our inheritance until the redemption of those who are God's possession.

—EPHESIANS 1:13-14

The Lord's arm is not too short to save

Surely the arm of the Lord is not too short to save, nor his ear too dull to hear.

—ISAIAH 59:1

Whoever believes in Jesus will be resurrected

I am the resurrection and the life. He who believes in me will live, even though he dies; and whoever lives and believes in me will never die.

—JOHN 11:25-26

Those who believe are God's children

To all who received him, to those who believed in his name, he gave the right to become children of God.

—JOHN 1:12

Salvation is a free gift rooted in God's grace

All have sinned and fall short of the glory of God, and are justified freely by his grace through the redemption that came by Christ Jesus.

— Romans 3:23-24

Faith is credited as righteousness

To the man who does not work but trusts God who justifies the wicked, his faith is credited as righteousness.

— Romans 4:5

E

Our bodies may age, but our spirits are renewed
We do not lose heart. Though outwardly we are wasting away, yet inwardly we are being renewed day by day.

—2 CORINTHIANS 4:16

The righteous bear fruit even in old age
The righteous will flourish like a palm tree, they will grow like a cedar of Lebanon; planted in the house of the Lord, they will flourish in the courts of our God. They will still bear fruit in old age, they will stay fresh and green.

—PSALM 92:12-14

God strengthens the weak
He gives strength to the weary and increases the power of the weak.

—ISAIAH 40:29

God is our guide to the very end of our lives
This God is our God for ever and ever; he will be our guide even to the end.

—PSALM 48:14

Encouragement

God's mercies are new each morning

Because of the Lord's great love we are not consumed, for his compassions never fail. They are new every morning.

— LAMENTATIONS 3:22-23

God renews those who hope in Him

Those who hope in the Lord will renew their strength. They will soar on wings like eagles; they will run and not grow weary, they will walk and not be faint.

— ISAIAH 40:31

The Lord sustains us in our troubles

Cast your cares on the Lord and he will sustain you.

— PSALM 55:22

The Lord is good to those who hope in Him

The Lord is good to those whose hope is in him, to the one who seeks him; it is good to wait quietly for the salvation of the Lord.

— LAMENTATIONS 3:25-26

Enemies

God guards those who fear Him
The angel of the Lord encamps around those who fear him, and he delivers them.

—Psalm 34:7

God delivers the faithful
He guards the lives of his faithful ones and delivers them from the hand of the wicked.

—Psalm 97:10

God delivers the righteous
The righteous cry out, and the Lord hears them; he delivers them from all their troubles.

—Psalm 34:17

God delivers those who call on Him
Call upon me in the day of trouble; I will deliver you, and you will honor me.

—Psalm 50:15

God is our powerful protector
He will cover you with his feathers, and under his wings you will find refuge; his faithfulness will be your shield and rampart. You will not fear the terror of night, nor the arrow that flies by day, nor the pestilence that stalks in the darkness, nor the plague that destroys at midday.

—Psalm 91:4-6

Eternal Life

Those who believe in Jesus receive eternal life

For God so loved the world that he gave his one and only Son, that whoever believes in him shall not perish but have eternal life.

—JOHN 3:16 (SEE ALSO JOHN 3:36)

Christians will be resurrected

I am the resurrection and the life. He who believes in me will live, even though he dies; and whoever lives and believes in me will never die.

—JOHN 11:25-26

He who has the Son has life

This is the testimony: God has given us eternal life, and this life is in his Son. He who has the Son has life; he who does not have the Son of God does not have life.

—1 JOHN 5:11-12

Eternal life is a gift of God

The wages of sin is death, but the gift of God is eternal life in Christ Jesus our Lord.

—ROMANS 6:23

The perishable will be made imperishable

The trumpet will sound, the dead will be raised imperishable, and we will be changed. For the perishable must clothe itself with the imperishable, and the mortal with immortality.

—1 CORINTHIANS 15:52-53

Tears and death will pass away

He will wipe every tear from their eyes. There will be no more death or mourning or crying or pain, for the old order of things has passed away.

—REVELATION 21:4

He will swallow up death forever. The Sovereign Lord will wipe away the tears from all faces.

—ISAIAH 25:8

Our eternal life is secure

My sheep listen to my voice; I know them, and they follow me. I give them eternal life, and they shall never perish; no one can snatch them out of my hand. My Father, who has given them to me, is greater than all; no one can snatch them out of my Father's hand.

—JOHN 10:27-29

Eternity

We will live with God face-to-face

Now the dwelling of God is with men, and he will live with

them. They will be his people, and God himself will be with them and be their God. He will wipe every tear from their eyes. There will be no more death or mourning or crying or pain, for the old order of things has passed away.

—REVELATION 21:3-4

Death will be swallowed up in victory

When the perishable has been clothed with the imperishable, and the mortal with immortality, then the saying that is written will come true: "Death has been swallowed up in victory."

—1 CORINTHIANS 15:54

A wonderful destiny awaits those who love God

No eye has seen, no ear has heard, no mind has conceived what God has prepared for those who love him.

—1 CORINTHIANS 2:9

Permanent resurrection bodies await us

We know that if the earthly tent we live in is destroyed, we have a building from God, an eternal house in heaven, not built by human hands.

—2 CORINTHIANS 5:1

F

Your work is not in vain

Let nothing move you. Always give yourselves fully to the work of the Lord, because you know that your labor in the Lord is not in vain.

—1 CORINTHIANS 15:58

Persevere, and you'll receive what God has promised

You need to persevere so that when you have done the will of God, you will receive what he has promised.

—HEBREWS 10:36

Stay confident, and you will be rewarded

Do not throw away your confidence; it will be richly rewarded. You need to persevere so that when you have done the will of God, you will receive what he has promised.

—HEBREWS 10:35-36

Faith

Faith in God can bring big results
Everything is possible for him who believes.

—MARK 9:23

I tell you the truth, if anyone says to this mountain, "Go, throw yourself into the sea," and does not doubt in his heart but believes that what he says will happen, it will be done for him.

—MARK 11:22-23

Even small faith brings big results
I tell you the truth, if you have faith as small as a mustard seed, you can say to this mountain, "Move from here to there" and it will move. Nothing will be impossible for you.

—MATTHEW 17:20 (SEE ALSO LUKE 17:6)

Those who have faith will do great things
I tell you the truth, anyone who has faith in me will do what I have been doing. He will do even greater things than these, because I am going to the Father.

—JOHN 14:12

The prayer of faith can bring healing
Is any one of you sick? He should call the elders of the church to pray over him and anoint him with oil in the name of

the Lord. And the prayer offered in faith will make the sick person well; the Lord will raise him up.

—JAMES 5:14-15

Hearing God's Word increases our faith

Faith comes from hearing the message, and the message is heard through the word of Christ.

—ROMANS 10:17

Faithfulness

God and His promises are faithful

Let us hold unswervingly to the hope we profess, for he who promised is faithful.

—HEBREWS 10:23

God is faithful even when we are faithless

If we are faithless, he will remain faithful, for he cannot disown himself.

—2 TIMOTHY 2:13

The Lord faithfully protects us

The Lord is faithful, and he will strengthen and protect you from the evil one.

—2 THESSALONIANS 3:3

God is faithful in showing compassion

Because of the Lord's great love we are not consumed, for his compassions never fail. They are new every morning; great is your faithfulness.

—LAMENTATIONS 3:22-23

God is faithful through all generations

The Lord is good and his love endures forever; his faithfulness continues through all generations.

—PSALM 100:5

God will faithfully bring about what He has promised

What I have said, that will I bring about; what I have planned, that will I do.

—ISAIAH 46:11 (SEE ALSO NUMBERS 23:19)

God is faithful to forgive us

If we confess our sins, he is faithful and just and will forgive us our sins and purify us from all unrighteousness.

—1 JOHN 1:9

Fear

God has given us a spirit of power, not fear

God did not give us a spirit of timidity, but a spirit of power, of love and of self-discipline.

—2 TIMOTHY 1:7

We are sons of God, not slaves to fear

Those who are led by the Spirit of God are sons of God. For you did not receive a spirit that makes you a slave again to fear, but you received the Spirit of sonship. And by him we cry, "Abba, Father."

—ROMANS 8:14-15

God is our refuge

God is our refuge and strength, an ever-present help in trouble.

—PSALM 46:1

God is our comforter, so we need not fear men

I, even I, am he who comforts you. Who are you that you fear mortal men, the sons of men, who are but grass?

—ISAIAH 51:12

The Lord is our helper, so we need not be afraid

We say with confidence, "The Lord is my helper; I will not be afraid. What can man do to me?"

—HEBREWS 13:6

God is our powerful protector

He will cover you with his feathers, and under his wings you will find refuge; his faithfulness will be your shield and rampart. You will not fear the terror of night, nor the arrow that flies by day, nor the pestilence that stalks in the darkness, nor the plague that destroys at midday.

—PSALM 91:4-6

Fear of the Lord

The Lord delights in those who fear Him
The Lord delights in those who fear him, who put their hope in his unfailing love.

—PSALM 147:11

The Lord provides for those who fear Him
Fear the Lord, you his saints, for those who fear him lack nothing.

—PSALM 34:9

The Lord's love is with those who fear Him
From everlasting to everlasting the Lord's love is with those who fear him, and his righteousness with their children's children.

—PSALM 103:17

The Lord has compassion on those who fear Him
As a father has compassion on his children, so the Lord has compassion on those who fear him.

—PSALM 103:13

The Lord fulfills the desires of those who fear Him

He fulfills the desires of those who fear him; he hears their cry and saves them.

—PSALM 145:19

The Lord watches over those who fear Him

The eyes of the Lord are on those who fear him, on those whose hope is in his unfailing love.

—PSALM 33:18

The Lord protects those who fear Him

The angel of the Lord encamps around those who fear him, and he delivers them.

—PSALM 34:7

Fellowship

Christ fellowships upon invitation

Here I am! I stand at the door and knock. If anyone hears my voice and opens the door, I will come in and eat with him, and he with me.

—REVELATION 3:20

The Lord is with those who gather in His name

If two of you on earth agree about anything you ask for, it

will be done for you by my Father in heaven. For where two or three come together in my name, there am I with them.

— MATTHEW 18:19-20

Those who love Jesus enjoy fellowship with God

If anyone loves me, he will obey my teaching. My Father will love him, and we will come to him and make our home with him.

— JOHN 14:23 (SEE ALSO JOHN 14:21)

We have fellowship with God if we walk in the light

If we claim to have fellowship with him yet walk in the darkness, we lie and do not live by the truth. But if we walk in the light, as he is in the light, we have fellowship with one another, and the blood of Jesus, his Son, purifies us from all sin.

— I JOHN 1:6-7

God lives in us if we love one another

No one has ever seen God; but if we love one another, God lives in us and his love is made complete in us.

— I JOHN 4:12

Finances

Seek God's kingdom, and He will provide basic needs

Do not worry, saying, "What shall we eat?" or "What shall

we drink?" or "What shall we wear?" For the pagans run after all these things, and your heavenly Father knows that you need them. But seek first his kingdom and his righteousness, and all these things will be given to you as well.

— MATTHEW 6:31-33

God will meet all our needs

My God will meet all your needs according to his glorious riches in Christ Jesus.

— PHILIPPIANS 4:19

Do not worry about your life, what you will eat; or about your body, what you will wear. Life is more than food, and the body more than clothes. Consider the ravens: They do not sow or reap, they have no storeroom or barn; yet God feeds them. And how much more valuable you are than birds!

— LUKE 12:22-24

God will never forsake you, so don't love money

Keep your lives free from the love of money and be content with what you have, because God has said, "Never will I leave you; never will I forsake you."

— HEBREWS 13:5

Give, and it will be given to you

Give, and it will be given to you. A good measure, pressed down, shaken together and running over, will be poured into your lap. For with the measure you use, it will be measured to you.

—LUKE 6:38

If you sow sparingly, you will reap sparingly

Whoever sows sparingly will also reap sparingly, and whoever sows generously will also reap generously. God is able to make all grace abound to you, so that in all things at all times, having all that you need, you will abound in every good work.

—2 CORINTHIANS 9:6,8

Food and Clothing

God will provide food and clothing

Do not worry about your life, what you will eat or drink; or about your body, what you will wear. Is not life more important than food, and the body more important than clothes? Look at the birds of the air; they do not sow or reap or store away in barns, and yet your heavenly Father feeds them. Are you not much more valuable than they?

—MATTHEW 6:25-26

God will provide clothing

If that is how God clothes the grass of the field, which is here today, and tomorrow is thrown into the fire, how much more will he clothe you, O you of little faith!

—LUKE 12:28

Seek God's kingdom, and He will meet basic needs

Do not worry, saying, "What shall we eat?" or "What shall we drink?" or "What shall we wear?" For the pagans run after all these things, and your heavenly Father knows that you need them. But seek first his kingdom and his righteousness, and all these things will be given to you as well.

—MATTHEW 6:31-33

God provides for those who fear Him

He provides food for those who fear him.

—PSALM 111:5

God will meet all our needs

My God will meet all your needs according to his glorious riches in Christ Jesus.

—PHILIPPIANS 4:19

Forgiveness

We are redeemed and forgiven

In him we have redemption through his blood, the forgiveness of sins, in accordance with the riches of God's grace.

—EPHESIANS 1:7

We are forgiven

He forgave us all our sins, having canceled the written code,

with its regulations, that was against us and that stood
opposed to us; he took it away, nailing it to the cross.

—COLOSSIANS 2:13-14

God cleanses the stain of sin from our souls
"Come now, let us reason together," says the Lord. "Though
your sins are like scarlet, they shall be as white as snow;
though they are red as crimson, they shall be like wool."

—ISAIAH 1:18

God completely removes our transgressions from us
As far as the east is from the west, so far has he removed our
transgressions from us.

—PSALM 103:12

God forgives our sins when we confess
If we confess our sins, he is faithful and just and will forgive
us our sins and purify us from all unrighteousness.

—1 JOHN 1:9

God forgives our wickedness
I will forgive their wickedness and will remember their sins
no more.

—HEBREWS 8:12

God forgives us as we forgive others
If you forgive men when they sin against you, your heavenly

Father will also forgive you. But if you do not forgive men their sins, your Father will not forgive your sins.

—MATTHEW 6:14-15 (SEE ALSO LUKE 6:37)

Freedom

Christ sets us free
It is for freedom that Christ has set us free. Stand firm, then, and do not let yourselves be burdened again by a yoke of slavery.

—GALATIANS 5:1

If the Son sets you free, you will be free indeed.

—JOHN 8:36

The truth sets us free
You will know the truth, and the truth will set you free.

—JOHN 8:32

Where the Spirit is, there is freedom
The Lord is the Spirit, and where the Spirit of the Lord is, there is freedom.

—2 CORINTHIANS 3:17

Sin shall not be your master
Sin shall not be your master, because you are not under law, but under grace.

—ROMANS 6:14

We are released from the law

By dying to what once bound us, we have been released from the law so that we serve in the new way of the Spirit, and not in the old way of the written code.

—ROMANS 7:6

Fresh Start

God's mercies are new every morning

Because of the Lord's great love we are not consumed, for his compassions never fail. They are new every morning.

—LAMENTATIONS 3:22-23

We are new creations in Christ

If anyone is in Christ, he is a new creation; the old has gone, the new has come!

—2 CORINTHIANS 5:17

Our spirits are renewed daily

We do not lose heart. Though outwardly we are wasting away, yet inwardly we are being renewed day by day.

—2 CORINTHIANS 4:16

Those who hope in the Lord receive renewed strength

Those who hope in the Lord will renew their strength. They will soar on wings like eagles; they will run and not grow weary, they will walk and not be faint.

—ISAIAH 40:31

With renewed minds we can discern God's will

Do not conform any longer to the pattern of this world, but be transformed by the renewing of your mind. Then you will be able to test and approve what God's will is—his good, pleasing and perfect will.

—ROMANS 12:2

Friendship of God

We are Christ's friends if we obey Him

You are my friends if you do what I command.

—JOHN 15:14

Obedience brings fellowship with God

If anyone loves me, he will obey my teaching. My Father will love him, and we will come to him and make our home with him.

—JOHN 14:23

Christ fellowships upon invitation

Here I am! I stand at the door and knock. If anyone hears my voice and opens the door, I will come in and eat with him, and he with me.

—REVELATION 3:20

The Lord is near to those who call on Him

The Lord is near to all who call on him, to all who call on him in truth.

—PSALM 145:18

God draws near to those who draw near to Him
Come near to God and he will come near to you.

—JAMES 4:8

Fruitfulness

The righteous bear fruit
The righteous will flourish like a palm tree, they will grow like a cedar of Lebanon; planted in the house of the Lord, they will flourish in the courts of our God. They will still bear fruit in old age, they will stay fresh and green.

—PSALM 92:12-14

Those who trust in the Lord bear fruit
Blessed is the man who trusts in the Lord, whose confidence is in him. He will be like a tree planted by the water that sends out its roots by the stream. It does not fear when heat comes; its leaves are always green. It has no worries in a year of drought and never fails to bear fruit.

—JEREMIAH 17:7-8

He who delights in God's Word bears fruit
Blessed is the man who does not walk in the counsel of the wicked or stand in the way of sinners or sit in the seat of mockers. But his delight is in the law of the Lord, and on his law he meditates day and night. He is like a tree planted by

streams of water, which yields its fruit in season and whose leaf does not wither. Whatever he does prospers.

—PSALM 1:1-3

Those who abide in Christ bear fruit

I am the vine; you are the branches. If a man remains in me and I in him, he will bear much fruit; apart from me you can do nothing.

—JOHN 15:5

Frustration

The Lord is our refuge

The Lord is good, a refuge in times of trouble. He cares for those who trust in him.

—NAHUM 1:7 (SEE ALSO PSALM 34:17)

The Lord will sustain us in our troubles

Cast your cares on the Lord and he will sustain you; he will never let the righteous fall.

—PSALM 55:22

Even in our troubles, God is working for our good

We know that in all things God works for the good of those who love him, who have been called according to his purpose.

—ROMANS 8:28

Perseverance yields the crown of life

Blessed is the man who perseveres under trial, because when he has stood the test, he will receive the crown of life that God has promised to those who love him.

—JAMES 1:12

The mind focused on God has perfect peace

You will keep in perfect peace him whose mind is steadfast, because he trusts in you.

—ISAIAH 26:3

A love for God's Word yields peace

Great peace have they who love your law, and nothing can make them stumble.

—PSALM 119:165

Fulfilled Life

Christ came to give us an abundant life

I have come that they may have life, and have it to the full.

—JOHN 10:10

God is the true source of satisfaction

He satisfies the thirsty and fills the hungry with good things.

—PSALM 107:9

Jesus satisfies spiritual hunger
Jesus declared, "I am the bread of life. He who comes to me will never go hungry, and he who believes in me will never be thirsty."

—JOHN 6:35

Everyone who drinks this water will be thirsty again, but whoever drinks the water I give him will never thirst. Indeed, the water I give him will become in him a spring of water welling up to eternal life.

—JOHN 4:13-14

Future

A wonderful destiny awaits those who love God
No eye has seen, no ear has heard, no mind has conceived what God has prepared for those who love him.

—I CORINTHIANS 2:9

Our citizenship is in heaven
Our citizenship is in heaven. And we eagerly await a Savior from there, the Lord Jesus Christ, who, by the power that enables him to bring everything under his control, will transform our lowly bodies so that they will be like his glorious body.

—PHILIPPIANS 3:20-21

Our perishable bodies will be made imperishable

The trumpet will sound, the dead will be raised imperishable, and we will be changed. For the perishable must clothe itself with the imperishable, and the mortal with immortality.

—1 CORINTHIANS 15:52-53

We will live with Christ

In my Father's house are many rooms.... I am going there to prepare a place for you. And if I go and prepare a place for you, I will come back and take you to be with me that you also may be where I am.

—JOHN 14:2-3

We are destined for glory

Dear friends, now we are children of God, and what we will be has not yet been made known. But we know that when he appears, we shall be like him, for we shall see him as he is.

—1 JOHN 3:2

When Christ, who is your life, appears, then you also will appear with him in glory.

—COLOSSIANS 3:4

G

Good comes to the generous

Good will come to him who is generous and lends freely,
who conducts his affairs with justice.

— PSALM 112:5

Give, and it will be given to you

Give, and it will be given to you. A good measure, pressed
down, shaken together and running over, will be poured into
your lap. For with the measure you use, it will be measured
to you.

— LUKE 6:38

If you sow generously, you will reap generously

Whoever sows sparingly will also reap sparingly, and whoever
sows generously will also reap generously.

— 2 CORINTHIANS 9:6

God is our supplier

Now he who supplies seed to the sower and bread for food

123

will also supply and increase your store of seed and will enlarge the harvest of your righteousness. You will be made rich in every way so that you can be generous on every occasion, and through us your generosity will result in thanksgiving to God.

—2 CORINTHIANS 9:10-11

Glory

Our sufferings pale in comparison to our future glory

I consider that our present sufferings are not worth comparing with the glory that will be revealed in us.

—ROMANS 8:18

Our future glory outweighs all present troubles

Our light and momentary troubles are achieving for us an eternal glory that far outweighs them all. So we fix our eyes not on what is seen, but on what is unseen. For what is seen is temporary, but what is unseen is eternal.

—2 CORINTHIANS 4:17-18

We will appear with Christ in glory

When Christ, who is your life, appears, then you also will appear with him in glory.

—COLOSSIANS 3:4

Our bodies will be gloriously transformed

Our citizenship is in heaven. And we eagerly await a Savior from there, the Lord Jesus Christ, who, by the power that enables him to bring everything under his control, will transform our lowly bodies so that they will be like his glorious body.

— PHILIPPIANS 3:20-21

God's Word

Scripture is inspired and leads us into truth

All Scripture is God-breathed and is useful for teaching, rebuking, correcting and training in righteousness, so that the man of God may be thoroughly equipped for every good work.

— 2 TIMOTHY 3:16-17

Obedience to God's Word yields blessing

The man who looks intently into the perfect law that gives freedom, and continues to do this, not forgetting what he has heard, but doing it—he will be blessed in what he does.

— JAMES 1:25

Meditating on God's Word brings success

Do not let this Book of the Law depart from your mouth; meditate on it day and night, so that you may be careful to do everything written in it. Then you will be prosperous and successful.

—JOSHUA 1:8

Those who love God's Word have peace

Great peace have they who love your law, and nothing can make them stumble.

—PSALM 119:165

Good News (Gospel)

Those who believe in Jesus receive eternal life

For God so loved the world that he gave his one and only Son, that whoever believes in him shall not perish but have eternal life.

—JOHN 3:16

We are brought near to God through Christ

In Christ Jesus you who once were far away have been brought near through the blood of Christ.

—EPHESIANS 2:13

Jesus took our sin and gave us His righteousness

God made him who had no sin to be sin for us, so that in him we might become the righteousness of God.

—2 CORINTHIANS 5:21

God loved us when we were still sinners

God demonstrates his own love for us in this: While we were still sinners, Christ died for us.

—ROMANS 5:8

We are forgiven

He forgave us all our sins, having canceled the written code, with its regulations, that was against us and that stood opposed to us; he took it away, nailing it to the cross.

—COLOSSIANS 2:13-14

Goodness

The Lord is good

The Lord is good, a refuge in times of trouble. He cares for those who trust in him.

—NAHUM 1:7

The Lord is good and his love endures forever; his faithfulness continues through all generations.

—PSALM 100:5

The Lord is good to all

The Lord is good to all; he has compassion on all he has made.

—PSALM 145:9

Even in our troubles, God is working for our good
We know that in all things God works for the good of
those who love him, who have been called according to his
purpose.

— ROMANS 8:28

God continues to do His good work in us
He who began a good work in you will carry it on to completion until the day of Christ Jesus.

— PHILIPPIANS 1:6

God has prepared good works for us to do
We are God's workmanship, created in Christ Jesus to do
good works, which God prepared in advance for us to do.

— EPHESIANS 2:10

Grace

We are saved by grace
Because of his great love for us, God, who is rich in mercy,
made us alive with Christ even when we were dead in transgressions—it is by grace you have been saved.

— EPHESIANS 2:4-5

It is by grace you have been saved, through faith—and this

not from yourselves, it is the gift of God—not by works, so that no one can boast.

—EPHESIANS 2:8-9

Our salvation demonstrates God's grace

God raised us up with Christ and seated us with him in the heavenly realms in Christ Jesus, in order that in the coming ages he might show the incomparable riches of his grace, expressed in his kindness to us in Christ Jesus.

—EPHESIANS 2:6-7

Christians enjoy a permanent standing in grace

Since we have been justified through faith, we have peace with God through our Lord Jesus Christ, through whom we have gained access by faith into this grace in which we now stand. And we rejoice in the hope of the glory of God.

—ROMANS 5:1-2

God gives you the grace you need to do good

God is able to make all grace abound to you, so that in all things at all times, having all that you need, you will abound in every good work.

—2 CORINTHIANS 9:8

The God of grace restores us

The God of all grace, who called you to his eternal glory

in Christ, after you have suffered a little while, will himself restore you and make you strong, firm and steadfast.

—1 PETER 5:10

Grief

The death of Christians is precious to God
Precious in the sight of the Lord is the death of his saints.

—PSALM 116:15

Death is not the end
We do not want you to be ignorant about those who fall asleep, or to grieve like the rest of men, who have no hope.... The dead in Christ will rise first. After that, we who are still alive and are left will be caught up together with them in the clouds to meet the Lord in the air. And so we will be with the Lord forever.

—1 THESSALONIANS 4:13-17

God comforts those who mourn
Blessed are those who mourn, for they will be comforted.

—MATTHEW 5:4

God will wipe away every tear in heaven
Now the dwelling of God is with men, and he will live with them. They will be his people, and God himself will be with

them and be their God. He will wipe every tear from their eyes. There will be no more death or mourning or crying or pain, for the old order of things has passed away.

—REVELATION 21:3-4

God comforts us in our hurts

Praise be to the God and Father of our Lord Jesus Christ, the Father of compassion and the God of all comfort, who comforts us in all our troubles, so that we can comfort those in any trouble with the comfort we ourselves have received from God.

—2 CORINTHIANS 1:3-4

Growth, Spiritual

God daily continues His work in us

He who began a good work in you will carry it on to completion until the day of Christ Jesus.

—PHILIPPIANS 1:6

We are molded in Christ's image

We, who with unveiled faces all reflect the Lord's glory, are being transformed into his likeness with ever-increasing glory, which comes from the Lord, who is the Spirit.

—2 CORINTHIANS 3:18

Our renewed minds can discern God's will

Do not conform any longer to the pattern of this world, but be transformed by the renewing of your mind. Then you will be able to test and approve what God's will is—his good, pleasing and perfect will.

—ROMANS 12:2

Guarded by God

The Lord protects those who fear Him

The angel of the Lord encamps around those who fear him, and he delivers them.

—PSALM 34:7

God is our powerful protector

He will cover you with his feathers, and under his wings you will find refuge; his faithfulness will be your shield and rampart. You will not fear the terror of night, nor the arrow that flies by day, nor the pestilence that stalks in the darkness, nor the plague that destroys at midday.

—PSALM 91:4-6

The Lord protects us from Satan

The Lord is faithful, and he will strengthen and protect you from the evil one.

—2 THESSALONIANS 3:3

Guidance

God will guide us

I will instruct you and teach you in the way you should go; I will counsel you and watch over you.

—PSALM 32:8

God is our guide to the very end of our lives

This God is our God for ever and ever; he will be our guide even to the end.

—PSALM 48:14

The Holy Spirit will guide us

The Counselor, the Holy Spirit, whom the Father will send in my name, will teach you all things and will remind you of everything I have said to you.

—JOHN 14:26

The Lord guides those who delight in Him

If the Lord delights in a man's way, he makes his steps firm; though he stumble, he will not fall, for the Lord upholds him with his hand.

—PSALM 37:23-24

Our renewed minds can discern God's will

Do not conform any longer to the pattern of this world, but be transformed by the renewing of your mind. Then you will be able to test and approve what God's will is—his good, pleasing and perfect will.

— ROMANS 12:2

======= Guilt =======

We are new creatures in Christ
If anyone is in Christ, he is a new creation; the old has gone, the new has come!

— 2 CORINTHIANS 5:17

Those in Christ are not condemned
There is now no condemnation for those who are in Christ Jesus.

— ROMANS 8:1

We are forgiven
He forgave us all our sins, having canceled the written code, with its regulations, that was against us and that stood opposed to us; he took it away, nailing it to the cross.

— COLOSSIANS 2:13-14

God blots out our transgressions
I, even I, am he who blots out your transgressions, for my own sake, and remembers your sins no more.

— ISAIAH 43:25

God completely removes our sins
As far as the east is from the west, so far has he removed our transgressions from us.

—PSALM 103:12

God will no longer remember our sins
I will forgive their wickedness and will remember their sins no more.

—HEBREWS 8:12

God forgives us when we confess
If we confess our sins, he is faithful and just and will forgive us our sins and purify us from all unrighteousness.

—1 JOHN 1:9

H

A wonderful destiny awaits those who love God

No eye has seen, no ear has heard, no mind has conceived what God has prepared for those who love him.

—1 Corinthians 2:9

God will one day abolish tears and death

He will wipe every tear from their eyes. There will be no more death or mourning or crying or pain, for the old order of things has passed away.

—Revelation 21:4

We can enjoy a perpetual Sabbath-rest

There remains, then, a Sabbath-rest for the people of God.

—Hebrews 4:9

Healing

The prayer of faith can make a sick person well

Is any one of you sick? He should call the elders of the church to pray over him and anoint him with oil in the name of the Lord. And the prayer offered in faith will make the sick person well; the Lord will raise him up.

—JAMES 5:14-15

Though outwardly wasting away, we are inwardly renewed

We do not lose heart. Though outwardly we are wasting away, yet inwardly we are being renewed day by day.

—2 CORINTHIANS 4:16

Permanent resurrection bodies await us

We know that if the earthly tent we live in is destroyed, we have a building from God, an eternal house in heaven, not built by human hands.

—2 CORINTHIANS 5:1

Heaven

A wonderful destiny awaits those who love God

No eye has seen, no ear has heard, no mind has conceived what God has prepared for those who love him.

—1 CORINTHIANS 2:9

God will one day abolish tears and death

He will wipe every tear from their eyes. There will be no

more death or mourning or crying or pain, for the old order of things has passed away.

—REVELATION 21:4

Heaven has plenty of room

In my Father's house are many rooms…. I am going there to prepare a place for you. And if I go and prepare a place for you, I will come back and take you to be with me that you also may be where I am.

—JOHN 14:2-3

All needs will be met in heaven

Never again will they hunger; never again will they thirst. The sun will not beat upon them, nor any scorching heat. For the Lamb at the center of the throne will be their shepherd; he will lead them to springs of living water. And God will wipe away every tear from their eyes.

—REVELATION 7:16-17

Nothing impure will enter heaven

Nothing impure will ever enter it, nor will anyone who does what is shameful or deceitful, but only those whose names are written in the Lamb's book of life.

—REVELATION 21:27

We will have glorious resurrection bodies in heaven

We know that if the earthly tent we live in is destroyed, we have a building from God, an eternal house in heaven, not built by human hands.

—2 Corinthians 5:1

Help

The Lord's arm is not too short to save
Surely the arm of the Lord is not too short to save, nor his ear too dull to hear.

—Isaiah 59:1

The Lord is a stronghold in times of trouble
The Lord is a refuge for the oppressed, a stronghold in times of trouble.

—Psalm 9:9 (see also Nahum 1:7)

Christ helps us in our temptations
Because he himself suffered when he was tempted, he is able to help those who are being tempted.

—Hebrews 2:18

God delivers those who cry out to Him
He will deliver the needy who cry out, the afflicted who have no one to help.

—Psalm 72:12

The Lord delivers the righteous from troubles
A righteous man may have many troubles, but the Lord delivers him from them all.

—Psalm 34:19

Disaster will not befall us
No harm will befall you, no disaster will come near your tent. For he will command his angels concerning you to guard you in all your ways.

—Psalm 91:10-11

Holy Spirit

God will pour out His Spirit in the last days
In the last days, God says, I will pour out my Spirit on all people. Your sons and daughters will prophesy, your young men will see visions, your old men will dream dreams.

—Acts 2:17

The Holy Spirit indwells us
Whoever believes in me, as the Scripture has said, streams of living water will flow from within him. By this he meant the Spirit, whom those who believed in him were later to receive. Up to that time the Spirit had not been given, since Jesus had not yet been glorified.

—John 7:38-39

Living in dependence on the Spirit brings victory
Live by the Spirit, and you will not gratify the desires of the sinful nature.

—GALATIANS 5:16

The Holy Spirit helps us by praying for us
The Spirit himself intercedes for us with groans that words cannot express.

—ROMANS 8:26

The Holy Spirit reminds us of the teachings of Jesus
The Counselor, the Holy Spirit, whom the Father will send in my name, will teach you all things and will remind you of everything I have said to you.

—JOHN 14:26

The Holy Spirit guides us
When he, the Spirit of truth, comes, he will guide you into all truth.

—JOHN 16:13

Home with the Lord

We will live with God face-to-face
Now the dwelling of God is with men, and he will live with

141

them. They will be his people, and God himself will be with them and be their God.

—REVELATION 21:3

We will live forever in the place Jesus has prepared for us

In my Father's house are many rooms; if it were not so, I would have told you. I am going there to prepare a place for you. And if I go and prepare a place for you, I will come back and take you to be with me that you also may be where I am.

—JOHN 14:2-3

We will dwell in a new heaven and a new earth

Then I saw a new heaven and a new earth, for the first heaven and the first earth had passed away, and there was no longer any sea. I saw the Holy City, the new Jerusalem, coming down out of heaven from God, prepared as a bride beautifully dressed for her husband.

—REVELATION 21:1-2

In keeping with his promise we are looking forward to a new heaven and a new earth, the home of righteousness.

—2 PETER 3:13

═══════════════ Hope ═══════════════

We have a living hope

Praise be to the God and Father of our Lord Jesus Christ! In his great mercy he has given us new birth into a living hope through the resurrection of Jesus Christ from the dead.

—1 PETER 1:3

The hope of salvation is our helmet

Since we belong to the day, let us be self-controlled, putting on faith and love as a breastplate, and the hope of salvation as a helmet. For God did not appoint us to suffer wrath but to receive salvation through our Lord Jesus Christ.

—1 THESSALONIANS 5:8-9

God delivers those whose hope is in His unfailing love

The eyes of the Lord are on those who fear him, on those whose hope is in his unfailing love.

—PSALM 33:18

Those who hope in the Lord renew their strength

Those who hope in the Lord will renew their strength. They will soar on wings like eagles; they will run and not grow weary, they will walk and not be faint.

—ISAIAH 40:31

Hospitality

Doing good to others is doing good to Christ

I tell you the truth, whatever you did for one of the least of these brothers of mine, you did for me.

—MATTHEW 25:40

Charitable kindness to children brings blessing

If anyone gives even a cup of cold water to one of these little ones because he is my disciple, I tell you the truth, he will certainly not lose his reward.

—MATTHEW 10:42

Showing hospitality to enemies brings a reward

Love your enemies, do good to them, and lend to them without expecting to get anything back. Then your reward will be great, and you will be sons of the Most High, because he is kind to the ungrateful and wicked.

—LUKE 6:35

Giving in secret brings a reward

When you give to the needy, do not let your left hand know what your right hand is doing, so that your giving may be in secret. Then your Father, who sees what is done in secret, will reward you.

—MATTHEW 6:3-4

Humility

The humble will be exalted

Whoever exalts himself will be humbled, and whoever humbles himself will be exalted.

—MATTHEW 23:12

The humble will be lifted up
Humble yourselves before the Lord, and he will lift you up.

—JAMES 4:10

Humble yourselves, therefore, under God's mighty hand, that he may lift you up in due time.

—1 PETER 5:6

The Lord sustains the humble
The Lord sustains the humble but casts the wicked to the ground.

—PSALM 147:6

Becoming humble like a child yields greatness
I tell you the truth, unless you change and become like little children, you will never enter the kingdom of heaven. Therefore, whoever humbles himself like this child is the greatest in the kingdom of heaven.

—MATTHEW 18:3-4

The humble are crowned with salvation
The Lord takes delight in his people; he crowns the humble with salvation.

—PSALM 149:4

The Lord guides the humble
He guides the humble in what is right and teaches them his way.

—PSALM 25:9

I

The prayer of faith will make a sick person well

Is any one of you sick? He should call the elders of the church to pray over him and anoint him with oil in the name of the Lord. And the prayer offered in faith will make the sick person well; the Lord will raise him up.

—JAMES 5:14-15

Though outwardly wasting away, we are inwardly renewed

We do not lose heart. Though outwardly we are wasting away, yet inwardly we are being renewed day by day.

—2 CORINTHIANS 4:16

God is our guide to the very end of our lives

This God is our God for ever and ever; he will be our guide even to the end.

—PSALM 48:14

Permanent resurrection bodies await us

We know that if the earthly tent we live in is destroyed, we have a building from God, an eternal house in heaven, not built by human hands.

—2 CORINTHIANS 5:1

Inheritance

We are heirs of God and co-heirs with Christ

The Spirit himself testifies with our spirit that we are God's children. Now if we are children, then we are heirs—heirs of God and co-heirs with Christ, if indeed we share in his sufferings in order that we may also share in his glory.

—ROMANS 8:16-17

We are heirs according to the promise

If you belong to Christ, then you are Abraham's seed, and heirs according to the promise.

—GALATIANS 3:29

Our inheritance can never perish, spoil, or fade

In his great mercy he has given us new birth into a living hope through the resurrection of Jesus Christ from the dead, and into an inheritance that can never perish, spoil or fade— kept in heaven for you.

—1 PETER 1:3-4

We will receive an inheritance as a reward

Whatever you do, work at it with all your heart, as working for the Lord, not for men, since you know that you will receive an inheritance from the Lord as a reward. It is the Lord Christ you are serving.

—COLOSSIANS 3:23-24

The Holy Spirit is a deposit guaranteeing our inheritance

Having believed, you were marked in him with a seal, the promised Holy Spirit, who is a deposit guaranteeing our inheritance until the redemption of those who are God's possession—to the praise of his glory.

—EPHESIANS 1:13-14

Integrity

God withholds nothing from those whose walk is blameless

The Lord God is a sun and shield; the Lord bestows favor and honor; no good thing does he withhold from those whose walk is blameless.

—PSALM 84:11

Those who yearn for righteousness will be filled

Blessed are those who hunger and thirst for righteousness, for they will be filled.

—MATTHEW 5:6

The fruit of righteousness is peace

The fruit of righteousness will be peace; the effect of righteousness will be quietness and confidence forever.

—ISAIAH 32:17

The upright enter peace

Those who walk uprightly enter into peace.

—ISAIAH 57:2

J

Whoever follows Jesus will never walk in darkness
I am the light of the world. Whoever follows me will never
walk in darkness, but will have the light of life.

—JOHN 8:12

We have peace with God through Jesus
Since we have been justified through faith, we have peace
with God through our Lord Jesus Christ.

—ROMANS 5:1

Those in Christ are not condemned
There is now no condemnation for those who are in Christ
Jesus.

—ROMANS 8:1

In Jesus we have redemption and forgiveness
In him we have redemption through his blood, the forgiveness of sins, in accordance with the riches of God's grace.

—EPHESIANS 1:7 (SEE ALSO 1 PETER 1:18-19)

We become God's children through faith in Jesus

You are all sons of God through faith in Christ Jesus.

—GALATIANS 3:26

God meets our needs according to His riches in Christ Jesus

My God will meet all your needs according to his glorious riches in Christ Jesus.

—PHILIPPIANS 4:19

If we acknowledge Jesus, He acknowledges us

Whoever acknowledges me before men, the Son of Man will also acknowledge him before the angels of God. But he who disowns me before men will be disowned before the angels of God.

—LUKE 12:8-9

===== Joy =====

Our names are written in heaven

Do not rejoice that the spirits submit to you, but rejoice that your names are written in heaven.

—LUKE 10:20

Those who sow in tears will reap joy

Those who sow in tears will reap with songs of joy. He who

goes out weeping, carrying seed to sow, will return with songs of joy, carrying sheaves with him.

—PSALM 126:5-6

Obey Christ, and you will experience joy

If you obey my commands, you will remain in my love, just as I have obeyed my Father's commands and remain in his love. I have told you this so that my joy may be in you and that your joy may be complete.

—JOHN 15:10-11

Ask in Jesus' name, and your joy will be complete

Until now you have not asked for anything in my name. Ask and you will receive, and your joy will be complete.

—JOHN 16:24

Justice

All God's ways are just

He is the Rock, his works are perfect, and all his ways are just. A faithful God who does no wrong, upright and just is he.

—DEUTERONOMY 32:4

The works of God's hands are just

The works of his hands are faithful and just; all his precepts are trustworthy.

—PSALM 111:7

The Lord is a God of justice

The Lord longs to be gracious to you; he rises to show you compassion. For the Lord is a God of justice. Blessed are all who wait for him!

—ISAIAH 30:18

The Lord loves the just

The Lord loves the just and will not forsake his faithful ones. They will be protected forever, but the offspring of the wicked will be cut off.

—PSALM 37:28

Good comes to him who conducts his affairs with justice

Good will come to him who is generous and lends freely, who conducts his affairs with justice.

—PSALM 112:5

The Lord brings justice for the oppressed

The Lord works righteousness and justice for all the oppressed.

—PSALM 103:6

Justification

We are justified in the name of Jesus

You were washed, you were sanctified, you were justified in

153

the name of the Lord Jesus Christ and by the Spirit of our God.

— 1 CORINTHIANS 6:11

Jesus took our sin and gave us His righteousness

God made him who had no sin to be sin for us, so that in him we might become the righteousness of God.

— 2 CORINTHIANS 5:21

Jesus was raised to life for our justification

He was delivered over to death for our sins and was raised to life for our justification.

— ROMANS 4:25

We are justified through faith

When a man works, his wages are not credited to him as a gift, but as an obligation. However, to the man who does not work but trusts God who justifies the wicked, his faith is credited as righteousness.

— ROMANS 4:4-5

Since we have been justified through faith, we have peace with God through our Lord Jesus Christ.

— ROMANS 5:1

Because we are justified, we are saved from God's wrath

Since we have now been justified by his blood, how much more shall we be saved from God's wrath through him!

— ROMANS 5:9

K

========= Kindness of God =========

The Lord has compassion on all

The Lord is good to all; he has compassion on all he has made.

—PSALM 145:9

The Lord has compassion on those who fear Him

As a father has compassion on his children, so the Lord has compassion on those who fear him.

—PSALM 103:13

God's mercies are new every morning

Because of the Lord's great love we are not consumed, for his compassions never fail. They are new every morning.

—LAMENTATIONS 3:22-23

We are saved because of God's kindness and mercy

When the kindness and love of God our Savior appeared, he saved us, not because of righteous things we had done, but because of his mercy. He saved us through the washing of rebirth and renewal by the Holy Spirit.

—TITUS 3:4-5

God's kindness is expressed in Jesus

God raised us up with Christ and seated us with him in the heavenly realms in Christ Jesus, in order that in the coming ages he might show the incomparable riches of his grace, expressed in his kindness to us in Christ Jesus.

—EPHESIANS 2:6-7

Kingdom of God

God's kingdom rules over all

The Lord has established his throne in heaven, and his kingdom rules over all.

—PSALM 103:19

God has brought us into His kingdom

He has rescued us from the dominion of darkness and brought us into the kingdom of the Son he loves, in whom we have redemption, the forgiveness of sins.

—COLOSSIANS 1:13-14

Seek God's kingdom first, and He will meet your needs

Seek first his kingdom and his righteousness, and all these things will be given to you as well.

—MATTHEW 6:33

Obedience leads to greatness in the kingdom

Anyone who breaks one of the least of these commandments and teaches others to do the same will be called least in the kingdom of heaven, but whoever practices and teaches these commands will be called great in the kingdom of heaven.

—MATTHEW 5:19

Humility leads to greatness in the kingdom

Whoever humbles himself like this child is the greatest in the kingdom of heaven.

—MATTHEW 18:4

L

Obedience to God's Word brings freedom

The man who looks intently into the perfect law that gives freedom, and continues to do this, not forgetting what he has heard, but doing it—he will be blessed in what he does.

—JAMES 1:25

The truth sets us free

You will know the truth, and the truth will set you free.

—JOHN 8:32

We are free from the law

There is now no condemnation for those who are in Christ Jesus, because through Christ Jesus the law of the Spirit of life set me free from the law of sin and death.

—ROMANS 8:1-2

The Spirit brings freedom

The Lord is the Spirit, and where the Spirit of the Lord is, there is freedom.

—2 CORINTHIANS 3:17

We may approach God with freedom
In him and through faith in him we may approach God with freedom and confidence.

— EPHESIANS 3:12

Life

You need not worry about your life
Do not worry about your life, what you will eat or drink; or about your body, what you will wear. Is not life more important than food, and the body more important than clothes? Look at the birds of the air; they do not sow or reap or store away in barns, and yet your heavenly Father feeds them. Are you not much more valuable than they?

— MATTHEW 6:25-26

Jesus satisfies spiritual hunger in life
Jesus declared, "I am the bread of life. He who comes to me will never go hungry, and he who believes in me will never be thirsty."

— JOHN 6:35

In Jesus we have the light of life
I am the light of the world. Whoever follows me will never walk in darkness, but will have the light of life.

— JOHN 8:12

God has given us eternal life in Jesus

This is the testimony: God has given us eternal life, and this life is in his Son. He who has the Son has life; he who does not have the Son of God does not have life.

—1 JOHN 5:11-12 (SEE ALSO JOHN 3:16)

The mind controlled by the Spirit is life and peace

The mind of sinful man is death, but the mind controlled by the Spirit is life and peace.

—ROMANS 8:6

Because of Jesus, we can live a new life

We were therefore buried with him through baptism into death in order that, just as Christ was raised from the dead through the glory of the Father, we too may live a new life.

—ROMANS 6:4

Our lives will never end

Jesus said to her, "I am the resurrection and the life. He who believes in me will live, even though he dies; and whoever lives and believes in me will never die."

—JOHN 11:25-26

Loneliness

Christ is always with us

Surely I am with you always, to the very end of the age.

—MATTHEW 28:20

God is always with us

God is our refuge and strength, an ever-present help in trouble.

—Psalm 46:1

God heals the brokenhearted

He heals the brokenhearted and binds up their wounds.

—Psalm 147:3

Nothing can separate us from the love of Christ

I am convinced that neither death nor life, neither angels nor demons, neither the present nor the future, nor any powers, neither height nor depth, nor anything else in all creation, will be able to separate us from the love of God that is in Christ Jesus our Lord.

—Romans 8:38-39

Longing

God fulfills the desires of those who fear Him

He fulfills the desires of those who fear him; he hears their cry and saves them.

—Psalm 145:19

Delight in the Lord, and He will give you your desires

Delight yourself in the Lord and he will give you the desires of your heart.

—Psalm 37:4

The Lord withholds nothing good from those whose walk is blameless

The Lord God is a sun and shield; the Lord bestows favor and honor; no good thing does he withhold from those whose walk is blameless.

—PSALM 84:11

Dependence on the Spirit brings victory over unholy desires

Live by the Spirit, and you will not gratify the desires of the sinful nature.

—GALATIANS 5:16

The desires of the world will pass away

The world and its desires pass away, but the man who does the will of God lives forever.

—1 JOHN 2:17

Lord Jesus

Those who believe in the Lord Jesus are saved

Believe in the Lord Jesus, and you will be saved—you and your household.

—ACTS 16:31

We have peace with God through the Lord Jesus

Since we have been justified through faith, we have peace with God through our Lord Jesus Christ.

—ROMANS 5:1

We are sanctified and justified in the Lord Jesus

You were washed, you were sanctified, you were justified in the name of the Lord Jesus Christ and by the Spirit of our God.

—1 CORINTHIANS 6:11

Confess Jesus as Lord, and you will be saved

If you confess with your mouth, "Jesus is Lord," and believe in your heart that God raised him from the dead, you will be saved. For it is with your heart that you believe and are justified, and it is with your mouth that you confess and are saved.

—ROMANS 10:9-10

Every tongue will confess Jesus as Lord

God exalted him to the highest place and gave him the name that is above every name, that at the name of Jesus every knee should bow, in heaven and on earth and under the earth, and every tongue confess that Jesus Christ is Lord, to the glory of God the Father.

—PHILIPPIANS 2:9-11

===== Love for God and Jesus =====

Those who love Jesus are loved by the Father
Whoever has my commands and obeys them, he is the one who loves me. He who loves me will be loved by my Father, and I too will love him and show myself to him.

—JOHN 14:21

Love and obedience lead to fellowship
If anyone loves me, he will obey my teaching. My Father will love him, and we will come to him and make our home with him.

—JOHN 14:23

God rescues those who love Him
"Because he loves me," says the Lord, "I will rescue him; I will protect him, for he acknowledges my name."

—PSALM 91:14

A wonderful destiny awaits those who love God
No eye has seen, no ear has heard, no mind has conceived what God has prepared for those who love him.

—I CORINTHIANS 2:9

Love of God

God's love and compassion never fail

Because of the Lord's great love we are not consumed, for his compassions never fail. They are new every morning.

— LAMENTATIONS 3:22-23

God proved His love for us

God demonstrates his own love for us in this: While we were still sinners, Christ died for us.

— ROMANS 5:8

Our salvation is rooted in God's love

For God so loved the world that he gave his one and only Son, that whoever believes in him shall not perish but have eternal life.

— JOHN 3:16 (SEE ALSO EPHESIANS 2:4-7)

Nothing can separate us from God's love

I am convinced that neither death nor life, neither angels nor demons, neither the present nor the future, nor any powers, neither height nor depth, nor anything else in all creation, will be able to separate us from the love of God that is in Christ Jesus our Lord.

— ROMANS 8:38-39

God's love is everlastingly with those who fear Him

From everlasting to everlasting the Lord's love is with those who fear him.

— PSALM 103:17

Love of Others

God lives in the one who loves

Since God so loved us, we also ought to love one another. No one has ever seen God; but if we love one another, God lives in us and his love is made complete in us.

— I JOHN 4:11-12

Whoever loves lives in the light

Whoever loves his brother lives in the light, and there is nothing in him to make him stumble.

— I JOHN 2:10

God is pleased when you do good to others

Do not forget to do good and to share with others, for with such sacrifices God is pleased.

— HEBREWS 13:16

Lust

The world and its desires are passing away

The world and its desires pass away, but the man who does the will of God lives forever.

— I JOHN 2:17

We were rescued from the world and its lusts

All of us also lived among them at one time, gratifying the cravings of our sinful nature and following its desires and thoughts. Like the rest, we were by nature objects of wrath. But because of his great love for us, God, who is rich in mercy, made us alive with Christ even when we were dead in transgressions—it is by grace you have been saved.

— EPHESIANS 2:3-5 (SEE ALSO TITUS 3:3-5)

God can deliver you from any temptation

No temptation has seized you except what is common to man. And God is faithful; he will not let you be tempted beyond what you can bear. But when you are tempted, he will also provide a way out so that you can stand up under it.

— 1 CORINTHIANS 10:13

Living in dependence on the Spirit brings victory

Live by the Spirit, and you will not gratify the desires of the sinful nature.

— GALATIANS 5:16

M

God is working in us to bring us to maturity

It is God who works in you to will and to act according to his good purpose.

— PHILIPPIANS 2:13

God will one day bring His work in us to completion

He who began a good work in you will carry it on to completion until the day of Christ Jesus.

— PHILIPPIANS 1:6

We are being transformed into Christ's likeness

We, who with unveiled faces all reflect the Lord's glory, are being transformed into his likeness with ever-increasing glory, which comes from the Lord, who is the Spirit.

— 2 CORINTHIANS 3:18

Our renewed minds can discern the will of God

Do not conform any longer to the pattern of this world, but

be transformed by the renewing of your mind. Then you will be able to test and approve what God's will is—his good, pleasing and perfect will.

—ROMANS 12:2

Meditation

Those who meditate on God's Word prosper

Blessed is the man who does not walk in the counsel of the wicked or stand in the way of sinners or sit in the seat of mockers. But his delight is in the law of the Lord, and on his law he meditates day and night. He is like a tree planted by streams of water, which yields its fruit in season and whose leaf does not wither. Whatever he does prospers.

—PSALM 1:1-3

Do not let this Book of the Law depart from your mouth; meditate on it day and night, so that you may be careful to do everything written in it. Then you will be prosperous and successful.

—JOSHUA 1:8

Meekness

The humble will be exalted

Whoever exalts himself will be humbled, and whoever humbles himself will be exalted.

—MATTHEW 23:12

The humble will be lifted up

Humble yourselves before the Lord, and he will lift you up.

— James 4:10 (see also 1 Peter 5:6)

The Lord sustains the humble

The Lord sustains the humble but casts the wicked to the ground.

— Psalm 147:6

Becoming humble like a child yields greatness

I tell you the truth, unless you change and become like little children, you will never enter the kingdom of heaven. Therefore, whoever humbles himself like this child is the greatest in the kingdom of heaven.

— Matthew 18:3-4

The humble are crowned with salvation

The Lord takes delight in his people; he crowns the humble with salvation.

— Psalm 149:4

The Lord guides the humble

He guides the humble in what is right and teaches them his way.

— Psalm 25:9

Mental Distress

The Lord will sustain us in our troubles

Cast your cares on the Lord and he will sustain you.

—Psalm 55:22

God did not give us a spirit of timidity

God did not give us a spirit of timidity, but a spirit of power, of love and of self-discipline.

—2 Timothy 1:7

Turning anxieties over to God yields perfect peace

Do not be anxious about anything, but in everything, by prayer and petition, with thanksgiving, present your requests to God. And the peace of God, which transcends all understanding, will guard your hearts and your minds in Christ Jesus.

—Philippians 4:6-7

Christ gives us rest

Come to me, all you who are weary and burdened, and I will give you rest.

—Matthew 11:28

A love for God's Word yields peace

Great peace have they who love your law, and nothing can make them stumble.

—Psalm 119:165

God heals the brokenhearted
He heals the brokenhearted and binds up their wounds.

— PSALM 147:3

Mercy

The Lord's mercy is abundant
The Lord is full of compassion and mercy.

— JAMES 5:11

God is rich in mercy
Because of his great love for us, God, who is rich in mercy, made us alive with Christ even when we were dead in transgressions—it is by grace you have been saved.

— EPHESIANS 2:4-5

God has mercy on those who fear Him
His mercy extends to those who fear him, from generation to generation.

— LUKE 1:50

God has compassion on those who fear Him
As a father has compassion on his children, so the Lord has compassion on those who fear him.

— PSALM 103:13

God saved us because of His mercy

He saved us, not because of righteous things we had done, but because of his mercy. He saved us through the washing of rebirth and renewal by the Holy Spirit.

—TITUS 3:5

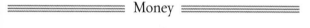

Money

We need not love money, for God will never forsake us

Keep your lives free from the love of money and be content with what you have, because God has said, "Never will I leave you; never will I forsake you."

—HEBREWS 13:5

God will meet all our needs

My God will meet all your needs according to his glorious riches in Christ Jesus.

—PHILIPPIANS 4:19

Do not worry about your life, what you will eat or drink; or about your body, what you will wear. Is not life more important than food, and the body more important than clothes? Look at the birds of the air; they do not sow or reap or store away in barns, and yet your heavenly Father feeds them. Are you not much more valuable than they?

—MATTHEW 6:25-26

N

Need

God will meet all our needs

My God will meet all your needs according to his glorious riches in Christ Jesus.

— PHILIPPIANS 4:19

God satisfies our needs

He satisfies the thirsty and fills the hungry with good things.

— PSALM 107:9

God provides food

He provides food for those who fear him.

— PSALM 111:5

The Lord delivers the needy

He will deliver the needy who cry out, the afflicted who have no one to help.

— PSALM 72:12

Seek God's kingdom first, and God will meet our needs

Do not worry, saying, "What shall we eat?" or "What shall we drink?" or "What shall we wear?" For the pagans run after all these things, and your heavenly Father knows that you need them. But seek first his kingdom and his righteousness, and all these things will be given to you as well.

—MATTHEW 6:31-33

God gives us what we need to do good

God is able to make all grace abound to you, so that in all things at all times, having all that you need, you will abound in every good work.

—2 CORINTHIANS 9:8

God gives us what we need for life and godliness

His divine power has given us everything we need for life and godliness through our knowledge of him who called us by his own glory and goodness.

—2 PETER 1:3

New Life

We are new creatures in Christ

If anyone is in Christ, he is a new creation; the old has gone, the new has come!

—2 CORINTHIANS 5:17

We have a new life in Jesus

We were therefore buried with him through baptism into death in order that, just as Christ was raised from the dead through the glory of the Father, we too may live a new life.

—ROMANS 6:4

Those who hope in the Lord will renew their strength

Those who hope in the Lord will renew their strength. They will soar on wings like eagles; they will run and not grow weary, they will walk and not be faint.

—ISAIAH 40:31

Our bodies may age, but our spirits are renewed daily

We do not lose heart. Though outwardly we are wasting away, yet inwardly we are being renewed day by day.

—2 CORINTHIANS 4:16

Obedience

God's love is made complete in the one who obeys

If anyone obeys his word, God's love is truly made complete in him. This is how we know we are in him.

—1 JOHN 2:5

Obedience brings the blessing of fellowship with God

If anyone loves me, he will obey my teaching. My Father will love him, and we will come to him and make our home with him.

—JOHN 14:23

God answers prayer when we obey Him

We have confidence before God and receive from him anything we ask, because we obey his commands and do what pleases him.

—1 JOHN 3:21-22

Obedience yields greatness in the kingdom

Anyone who breaks one of the least of these commandments

and teaches others to do the same will be called least in the kingdom of heaven, but whoever practices and teaches these commands will be called great in the kingdom of heaven.

—MATTHEW 5:19

Those who do God's will are members of His family
Whoever does the will of my Father in heaven is my brother and sister and mother.

—MATTHEW 12:50

Those who obey Jesus never permanently die
I tell you the truth, if anyone keeps my word, he will never see death.

—JOHN 8:51

P

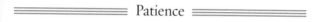 Patience

You will reap a harvest

Let us not become weary in doing good, for at the proper time we will reap a harvest if we do not give up.

—GALATIANS 6:9

You will receive a crown of life

Blessed is the man who perseveres under trial, because when he has stood the test, he will receive the crown of life that God has promised to those who love him.

—JAMES 1:12

Those who persevere will receive what God promised

You need to persevere so that when you have done the will of God, you will receive what he has promised.

—HEBREWS 10:36

The Lord is patient regarding salvation

The Lord is not slow in keeping his promise, as some

understand slowness. He is patient with you, not wanting anyone to perish, but everyone to come to repentance.

—2 PETER 3:9

Peace

Peacemakers are blessed
Blessed are the peacemakers, for they will be called sons of God.

—MATTHEW 5:9

Turning anxieties over to God yields perfect peace
Do not be anxious about anything, but in everything, by prayer and petition, with thanksgiving, present your requests to God. And the peace of God, which transcends all understanding, will guard your hearts and your minds in Christ Jesus.

—PHILIPPIANS 4:6-7

The mind focused on God has perfect peace
You will keep in perfect peace him whose mind is steadfast, because he trusts in you.

—ISAIAH 26:3

Christ gives us peace
Peace I leave with you; my peace I give you. I do not give to

you as the world gives. Do not let your hearts be troubled and do not be afraid.

—JOHN 14:27

A love for God's Word yields peace
Great peace have they who love your law, and nothing can make them stumble.

—PSALM 119:165

The mind controlled by the Spirit is life and peace
The mind of sinful man is death, but the mind controlled by the Spirit is life and peace.

—ROMANS 8:6

===== Persecution =====

Those persecuted for righteousness are blessed
Blessed are those who are persecuted because of righteousness, for theirs is the kingdom of heaven.

—MATTHEW 5:10

Those persecuted for following Jesus are blessed
Blessed are you when people insult you, persecute you and falsely say all kinds of evil against you because of me. Rejoice and be glad, because great is your reward in heaven.

—MATTHEW 5:11-12

Nothing can separate us from the love of Christ

I am convinced that neither death nor life, neither angels nor demons, neither the present nor the future, nor any powers, neither height nor depth, nor anything else in all creation, will be able to separate us from the love of God that is in Christ Jesus our Lord.

—ROMANS 8:38-39

We are blessed for suffering for what is right

Even if you should suffer for what is right, you are blessed.

—I PETER 3:14

We are blessed when insulted for serving Christ

If you are insulted because of the name of Christ, you are blessed, for the Spirit of glory and of God rests on you.

—I PETER 4:14

Perseverance

Perseverance yields the crown of life

Blessed is the man who perseveres under trial, because when he has stood the test, he will receive the crown of life that God has promised to those who love him.

—JAMES 1:12

Persevere, and you'll receive what God has promised

You need to persevere so that when you have done the will of
God, you will receive what he has promised.

—HEBREWS 10:36

Suffering produces perseverance

We also rejoice in our sufferings, because we know that suffering produces perseverance.

—ROMANS 5:3

Those who persevere will reap a harvest

Let us not become weary in doing good, for at the proper
time we will reap a harvest if we do not give up.

—GALATIANS 6:9

Prayer

Ask, and it will be given to you

Ask and it will be given to you; seek and you will find; knock
and the door will be opened to you. For everyone who asks
receives; he who seeks finds; and to him who knocks, the
door will be opened.

—MATTHEW 7:7-8 (SEE ALSO LUKE 11:9-10)

Pray in Jesus' name, and He will answer

I will do whatever you ask in my name, so that the Son may

183

bring glory to the Father. You may ask me for anything in my name, and I will do it.

—JOHN 14:13-14

God answers prayer when we obey

We have confidence before God and receive from him anything we ask, because we obey his commands and do what pleases him.

—1 JOHN 3:21-22

God answers prayer when we believe

I tell you the truth, if anyone says to this mountain, "Go, throw yourself into the sea," and does not doubt in his heart but believes that what he says will happen, it will be done for him. Therefore I tell you, whatever you ask for in prayer, believe that you have received it, and it will be yours.

—MARK 11:23-24 (SEE ALSO MATTHEW 21:22)

God answers the prayers of the righteous

The eyes of the Lord are on the righteous and his ears are attentive to their prayer, but the face of the Lord is against those who do evil.

—1 PETER 3:12

God answers prayer when we abide in Christ

If you remain in me and my words remain in you, ask whatever you wish, and it will be given you.

—JOHN 15:7

God answers prayers that are in accordance with His will

This is the confidence we have in approaching God: that if we ask anything according to his will, he hears us. And if we know that he hears us—whatever we ask—we know that we have what we asked of him.

—1 JOHN 5:14-15

God answers prayer when two or more agree

If two of you on earth agree about anything you ask for, it will be done for you by my Father in heaven. For where two or three come together in my name, there am I with them.

—MATTHEW 18:19-20

Presence of God

God will never leave us

Never will I leave you; never will I forsake you.

—HEBREWS 13:5

Christ is always with us

Surely I am with you always, to the very end of the age.

—MATTHEW 28:20

God will draw near to those who draw near to Him

Come near to God and he will come near to you.

—JAMES 4:8

We have fellowship when we walk in the light

If we walk in the light, as he is in the light, we have fellowship with one another, and the blood of Jesus, his Son, purifies us from all sin.

—1 JOHN 1:7

Christ will fellowship upon invitation

Here I am! I stand at the door and knock. If anyone hears my voice and opens the door, I will come in and eat with him, and he with me.

—REVELATION 3:20

Pride

God gives grace to the humble

All of you, clothe yourselves with humility toward one another, because, "God opposes the proud but gives grace to the humble." Humble yourselves, therefore, under God's mighty hand, that he may lift you up in due time.

—1 PETER 5:5-6 (SEE ALSO JAMES 4:6)

Those who exalt themselves will be humbled

Whoever exalts himself will be humbled, and whoever humbles himself will be exalted.

—MATTHEW 23:12 (SEE ALSO JAMES 4:10; 1 PETER 5:6)

Becoming humble like a child yields greatness

I tell you the truth, unless you change and become like little children, you will never enter the kingdom of heaven. Therefore, whoever humbles himself like this child is the greatest in the kingdom of heaven.

—MATTHEW 18:3-4

Following the humble Jesus yields rest

Take my yoke upon you and learn from me, for I am gentle and humble in heart, and you will find rest for your souls.

—MATTHEW 11:29

Priorities

Seek God's kingdom first, and He will provide basic needs

Seek first his kingdom and his righteousness, and all these things will be given to you as well.

—MATTHEW 6:33

Whoever loses his life for Jesus will find it

Whoever wants to save his life will lose it, but whoever loses his life for me will save it. What good is it for a man to gain the whole world, and yet lose or forfeit his very self?

—LUKE 9:24-25

Protection

God is our shield and rampart

He will cover you with his feathers, and under his wings you will find refuge; his faithfulness will be your shield and rampart. You will not fear the terror of night, nor the arrow that flies by day, nor the pestilence that stalks in the darkness, nor the plague that destroys at midday.

—PSALM 91:4-6 (SEE ALSO PSALM 18:30)

God rescues those who love Him

"Because he loves me," says the Lord, "I will rescue him; I will protect him, for he acknowledges my name."

—PSALM 91:14

The Lord protects His faithful ones

The Lord loves the just and will not forsake his faithful ones. They will be protected forever, but the offspring of the wicked will be cut off.

—PSALM 37:28

God protects us from Satan

The Lord is faithful, and he will strengthen and protect you from the evil one.

—2 THESSALONIANS 3:3

God protects us from disaster

If you make the Most High your dwelling—even the Lord, who is my refuge—then no harm will befall you, no disaster will come near your tent.

—PSALM 91:9-10

The Lord will watch over you

The Lord will keep you from all harm—he will watch over your life; the Lord will watch over your coming and going both now and forevermore.

—PSALM 121:7-8 (SEE ALSO PSALM 145:20)

Providence of God

The Lord's kingdom rules over all

The Lord has established his throne in heaven, and his kingdom rules over all.

—PSALM 103:19

The sovereign Lord rules

The Sovereign Lord comes with power, and his arm rules for him.

—ISAIAH 40:10

Even in our troubles, God is working for our good

We know that in all things God works for the good of those who love him, who have been called according to his purpose.

—ROMANS 8:28

Provision

God will meet all our needs

My God will meet all your needs according to his glorious riches in Christ Jesus.

—PHILIPPIANS 4:19

God provides for those who fear Him
He provides food for those who fear him.

—Psalm 111:5

Put God first, and temporal needs will be met
Seek first his kingdom and his righteousness, and all these things will be given to you as well.

—Matthew 6:33

God provides for our hunger
He satisfies the thirsty and fills the hungry with good things.

—Psalm 107:9

God will take care of you
If that is how God clothes the grass of the field, which is here today, and tomorrow is thrown into the fire, how much more will he clothe you, O you of little faith!

—Luke 12:28

Punishment

God lovingly disciplines Christians
"The Lord disciplines those he loves, and he punishes everyone he accepts as a son." Endure hardship as discipline; God is treating you as sons.

—Hebrews 12:6-7

God punishes the evil with everlasting destruction

They will be punished with everlasting destruction and shut out from the presence of the Lord and from the majesty of his power.

— 2 Thessalonians 1:9

Purification

God will cleanse the stain of sin from your soul

Though your sins are like scarlet, they shall be as white as snow; though they are red as crimson, they shall be like wool.

— Isaiah 1:18

The blood of Christ cleanses us

How much more, then, will the blood of Christ, who through the eternal Spirit offered himself unblemished to God, cleanse our consciences from acts that lead to death, so that we may serve the living God!

— Hebrews 9:14

We are purified from all sin

If we walk in the light, as he is in the light, we have fellowship with one another, and the blood of Jesus, his Son, purifies us from all sin.

— 1 John 1:7

God cleanses us when we confess
If we confess our sins, he is faithful and just and will forgive us our sins and purify us from all unrighteousness.

—1 John 1:9

Purity comes from following God's Word
How can a young man keep his way pure? By living according to your word.

—Psalm 119:9

The pure in heart will see God
Blessed are the pure in heart, for they will see God.

—Matthew 5:8

===== Pursuit of God =====

Seek God's kingdom first, and He will provide basic needs
Seek first his kingdom and his righteousness, and all these things will be given to you as well.

—Matthew 6:33

Seek God with all your heart and you will find Him
You will seek me and find me when you seek me with all your heart.

—Jeremiah 29:13

The Lord is good to the one who seeks Him

The Lord is good to those whose hope is in him, to the one who seeks him.

—LAMENTATIONS 3:25

Those who seek the Lord lack no good thing

The lions may grow weak and hungry, but those who seek the Lord lack no good thing.

—PSALM 34:10

God rewards those who earnestly seek Him

Without faith it is impossible to please God, because anyone who comes to him must believe that he exists and that he rewards those who earnestly seek him.

—HEBREWS 11:6

Seek and you will find

Ask and it will be given to you; seek and you will find; knock and the door will be opened to you. For everyone who asks receives; he who seeks finds; and to him who knocks, the door will be opened.

—MATTHEW 7:7-8 (SEE ALSO LUKE 11:9-10)

Q-R

We will all be changed

We will not all sleep, but we will all be changed—in a flash, in the twinkling of an eye, at the last trumpet. For the trumpet will sound, the dead will be raised imperishable, and we will be changed. For the perishable must clothe itself with the imperishable, and the mortal with immortality.

—1 Corinthians 15:51-53

We will meet the Lord in the clouds

The Lord himself will come down from heaven, with a loud command, with the voice of the archangel and with the trumpet call of God, and the dead in Christ will rise first. After that, we who are still alive and are left will be caught up together with them in the clouds to meet the Lord in the air. And so we will be with the Lord forever.

—1 Thessalonians 4:16-17

Rebirth

We are born again

You have been born again, not of perishable seed, but of

imperishable, through the living and enduring word of God.

—1 Peter 1:23

We are new creations in Christ

If anyone is in Christ, he is a new creation; the old has gone, the new has come!

—2 Corinthians 5:17

We are saved through the washing of rebirth

He saved us, not because of righteous things we had done, but because of his mercy. He saved us through the washing of rebirth and renewal by the Holy Spirit.

—Titus 3:5

Those who believe in Jesus are God's children

To all who received him, to those who believed in his name, he gave the right to become children of God.

—John 1:12

Redemption

We were redeemed by Jesus' blood

It was not with perishable things such as silver or gold that you were redeemed from the empty way of life handed down

to you from your forefathers, but with the precious blood of
Christ, a lamb without blemish or defect.

—1 PETER 1:18-19

We are redeemed and forgiven
In him we have redemption through his blood, the forgiveness of sins, in accordance with the riches of God's grace.

—EPHESIANS 1:7

Jesus died for the sins of the whole world
He is the atoning sacrifice for our sins, and not only for ours
but also for the sins of the whole world.

—1 JOHN 2:2 (SEE ALSO HEBREWS 9:28)

We are saved from God's wrath
Since we have now been justified by his blood, how much
more shall we be saved from God's wrath through him!

—ROMANS 5:9

We've been brought into a new kingdom
He has rescued us from the dominion of darkness and
brought us into the kingdom of the Son he loves, in whom
we have redemption, the forgiveness of sins.

—COLOSSIANS 1:13-14 (SEE ALSO COLOSSIANS 2:13-14)

Refreshment

God refreshes the weary

I will refresh the weary and satisfy the faint.

—JEREMIAH 31:25

Christ gives us rest

Come to me, all you who are weary and burdened, and I will give you rest.

—MATTHEW 11:28

Repentance brings times of refreshing

Repent, then, and turn to God, so that your sins may be wiped out, that times of refreshing may come from the Lord.

—ACTS 3:19

We are new creations in Christ

If anyone is in Christ, he is a new creation; the old has gone, the new has come!

—2 CORINTHIANS 5:17

Our spirits are renewed daily

We do not lose heart. Though outwardly we are wasting away, yet inwardly we are being renewed day by day.

—2 CORINTHIANS 4:16

Those who hope in the Lord will renew their strength

Those who hope in the Lord will renew their strength. They will soar on wings like eagles; they will run and not grow weary, they will walk and not be faint.

—ISAIAH 40:31

Repentance

Repentance leads to life

If a wicked man turns away from all the sins he has committed and keeps all my decrees and does what is just and right, he will surely live; he will not die. None of the offenses he has committed will be remembered against him. Because of the righteous things he has done, he will live.

—EZEKIEL 18:21-22

Repentance brings times of refreshing

Repent, then, and turn to God, so that your sins may be wiped out, that times of refreshing may come from the Lord.

—ACTS 3:19

Heaven rejoices when a sinner repents

There will be more rejoicing in heaven over one sinner who repents than over ninety-nine righteous persons who do not need to repent.

—LUKE 15:7 (SEE ALSO LUKE 15:10)

The Lord seeks all to come to repentance

The Lord is not slow in keeping his promise, as some understand slowness. He is patient with you, not wanting anyone to perish, but everyone to come to repentance.

—2 PETER 3:9

Christ gives us rest

Come to me, all you who are weary and burdened, and I will give you rest.

—MATTHEW 11:28

We can rest in the secure presence of God

He who dwells in the shelter of the Most High will rest in the shadow of the Almighty.

—PSALM 91:1

God refreshes the weary

I will refresh the weary and satisfy the faint.

—JEREMIAH 31:25

We can enjoy a perpetual Sabbath-rest

There remains, then, a Sabbath-rest for the people of God.

—HEBREWS 4:9 (SEE ALSO HEBREWS 4:1)

Restoration

We are new creatures in Christ
If anyone is in Christ, he is a new creation; the old has gone, the new has come!

— 2 CORINTHIANS 5:17

The Lord lifts up those who are bowed down
The Lord upholds all those who fall and lifts up all who are bowed down.

— PSALM 145:14

The God of grace will restore us
The God of all grace, who called you to his eternal glory in Christ, after you have suffered a little while, will himself restore you and make you strong, firm and steadfast.

— 1 PETER 5:10

Our spirits are renewed daily
We do not lose heart. Though outwardly we are wasting away, yet inwardly we are being renewed day by day.

— 2 CORINTHIANS 4:16

Those who hope in the Lord will renew their strength
Those who hope in the Lord will renew their strength. They will soar on wings like eagles; they will run and not grow weary, they will walk and not be faint.

— ISAIAH 40:31

We are brought near to God through Jesus Christ
In Christ Jesus you who once were far away have been brought near through the blood of Christ.

— EPHESIANS 2:13

Resurrection

Those who believe in Jesus will be resurrected
Jesus said to her, "I am the resurrection and the life. He who believes in me will live, even though he dies; and whoever lives and believes in me will never die."

— JOHN 11:25-26

We have a living hope of resurrection
Praise be to the God and Father of our Lord Jesus Christ! In his great mercy he has given us new birth into a living hope through the resurrection of Jesus Christ from the dead.

— 1 PETER 1:3

Our mortal bodies will be enlivened
If the Spirit of him who raised Jesus from the dead is living in you, he who raised Christ from the dead will also give life to your mortal bodies through his Spirit, who lives in you.

— ROMANS 8:11

Permanent resurrection bodies await us
We know that if the earthly tent we live in is destroyed, we

have a building from God, an eternal house in heaven, not built by human hands.

—2 CORINTHIANS 5:1

Our perishable bodies will be made imperishable
The body that is sown is perishable, it is raised imperishable; it is sown in dishonor, it is raised in glory; it is sown in weakness, it is raised in power; it is sown a natural body, it is raised a spiritual body.

—1 CORINTHIANS 15:42-44
(SEE ALSO 1 CORINTHIANS 15:51-53)

Some will rise to eternal life, others to everlasting contempt
A time is coming when all who are in their graves will hear his voice and come out—those who have done good will rise to live, and those who have done evil will rise to be condemned.

—JOHN 5:28-29 (SEE ALSO DANIEL 12:2)

Reward

The Lord will reward people for the good they do
The Lord will reward everyone for whatever good he does, whether he is slave or free.

—EPHESIANS 6:8

The Lord searches the heart to reward justly

I the Lord search the heart and examine the mind, to reward a man according to his conduct, according to what his deeds deserve.

—JEREMIAH 17:10

Even small acts of kindness will be rewarded

If anyone gives even a cup of cold water to one of these little ones because he is my disciple, I tell you the truth, he will certainly not lose his reward.

—MATTHEW 10:42

Enduring persecution for following Christ brings a reward

Blessed are you when people insult you, persecute you and falsely say all kinds of evil against you because of me. Rejoice and be glad, because great is your reward in heaven.

—MATTHEW 5:11-12

Persevering under trial brings a reward

Blessed is the man who perseveres under trial, because when he has stood the test, he will receive the crown of life that God has promised to those who love him.

—JAMES 1:12

We have an inheritance from the Lord as a reward

Whatever you do, work at it with all your heart, as working

for the Lord, not for men, since you know that you will receive an inheritance from the Lord as a reward. It is the Lord Christ you are serving.

—COLOSSIANS 3:23-24

Righteousness

The Lord is righteous
The Lord is righteous in all his ways and loving toward all he has made.

—PSALM 145:17

God blesses those who walk in righteousness
The Lord God is a sun and shield; the Lord bestows favor and honor; no good thing does he withhold from those whose walk is blameless.

—PSALM 84:11

Those who yearn for righteousness will be satisfied
Blessed are those who hunger and thirst for righteousness, for they will be filled.

—MATTHEW 5:6

God gives you what you need to be righteous
God is able to make all grace abound to you, so that in all

things at all times, having all that you need, you will abound in every good work.

—2 CORINTHIANS 9:8

Faith is credited as righteousness

To the man who does not work but trusts God who justifies the wicked, his faith is credited as righteousness.

—ROMANS 4:5 (SEE ALSO ROMANS 3:22-24; 5:17)

S

=== Sadness ===

God comforts those who mourn
Blessed are those who mourn, for they will be comforted.

—MATTHEW 5:4

God heals the brokenhearted
He heals the brokenhearted and binds up their wounds.

—PSALM 147:3

The Lord sustains us in our troubles
Cast your cares on the Lord and he will sustain you; he will never let the righteous fall.

—PSALM 55:22

God comforts us in all our troubles
Praise be to the God and Father of our Lord Jesus Christ, the Father of compassion and the God of all comfort, who comforts us in all our troubles, so that we can comfort those in any trouble with the comfort we ourselves have received from God.

—2 CORINTHIANS 1:3

God will help you

Do not fear, for I am with you; do not be dismayed, for I am your God. I will strengthen you and help you; I will uphold you with my righteous right hand.

— ISAIAH 41:10

Turning our anxieties over to God yields perfect peace

Do not be anxious about anything, but in everything, by prayer and petition, with thanksgiving, present your requests to God. And the peace of God, which transcends all understanding, will guard your hearts and your minds in Christ Jesus.

— PHILIPPIANS 4:6-7

Salvation

Those who believe in Jesus receive eternal life

For God so loved the world that he gave his one and only Son, that whoever believes in him shall not perish but have eternal life.

— JOHN 3:16 (SEE ALSO JOHN 3:36; 5:24; 6:47)

Those who believe in Jesus are God's children

To all who received him, to those who believed in his name, he gave the right to become children of God.

— JOHN 1:12

Those who believe in Jesus are saved

Believe in the Lord Jesus, and you will be saved—you and your household.

—ACTS 16:31

Eternal life is in the Son

This is the testimony: God has given us eternal life, and this life is in his Son. He who has the Son has life; he who does not have the Son of God does not have life.

—1 JOHN 5:11-12

Call on the name of the Lord, and you'll be saved

Everyone who calls on the name of the Lord will be saved.

—ACTS 2:21 (SEE ALSO ROMANS 10:11-13)

Confess, and you'll be saved

If you confess with your mouth, "Jesus is Lord," and believe in your heart that God raised him from the dead, you will be saved.

—ROMANS 10:9

Salvation, Security in

God's people are sealed by the Holy Spirit

Having believed, you were marked in him with a seal, the promised Holy Spirit, who is a deposit guaranteeing our inheritance until the redemption of those who are God's possession.

—EPHESIANS 1:13-14

Jesus prays for us

He is able to save completely those who come to God through him, because he always lives to intercede for them.

—HEBREWS 7:25

Christ will never reject any who come to Him

All that the Father gives me will come to me, and whoever comes to me I will never drive away.

—JOHN 6:37

No one can snatch believers out of God's hands

My sheep listen to my voice; I know them, and they follow me. I give them eternal life, and they shall never perish; no one can snatch them out of my hand. My Father, who has given them to me, is greater than all; no one can snatch them out of my Father's hand.

—JOHN 10:27-29

Salvation involves an unbroken chain

For those God foreknew he also predestined to be conformed to the likeness of his Son, that he might be the firstborn among many brothers. And those he predestined, he also called; those he called, he also justified; those he justified, he also glorified.

—ROMANS 8:29-30

Sanctification

Dependence on the Holy Spirit brings victory
Live by the Spirit, and you will not gratify the desires of the sinful nature.

—GALATIANS 5:16

The mind controlled by the Spirit is life and peace
Those who live according to the sinful nature have their minds set on what that nature desires; but those who live in accordance with the Spirit have their minds set on what the Spirit desires. The mind of sinful man is death, but the mind controlled by the Spirit is life and peace.

—ROMANS 8:5-6

We are being transformed into Christ's likeness
We, who with unveiled faces all reflect the Lord's glory, are being transformed into his likeness with ever-increasing glory, which comes from the Lord, who is the Spirit.

—2 CORINTHIANS 3:18

You can be transformed by the renewing of your mind
Do not conform any longer to the pattern of this world, but
be transformed by the renewing of your mind. Then you will
be able to test and approve what God's will is—his good,
pleasing and perfect will.

— ROMANS 12:2

We have been sanctified in the name of Jesus Christ
You were washed, you were sanctified, you were justified in
the name of the Lord Jesus Christ and by the Spirit of our
God.

— 1 CORINTHIANS 6:11

Satan

God will protect us from Satan
The Lord is faithful, and he will strengthen and protect you
from the evil one.

— 2 THESSALONIANS 3:3

God's armor protects us from Satan
Put on the full armor of God, so that when the day of evil
comes, you may be able to stand your ground, and after you
have done everything, to stand.

— EPHESIANS 6:13

Resist the devil, and he will flee from you
Resist the devil, and he will flee from you.

—JAMES 4:7

God will crush Satan
The God of peace will soon crush Satan under your feet.

—ROMANS 16:20

God is our powerful protector
He will cover you with his feathers, and under his wings you will find refuge; his faithfulness will be your shield and rampart. You will not fear the terror of night, nor the arrow that flies by day, nor the pestilence that stalks in the darkness, nor the plague that destroys at midday.

—PSALM 91:4-6

Satisfaction

Those who seek the Lord lack no good thing
The lions may grow weak and hungry, but those who seek the Lord lack no good thing.

—PSALM 34:10

Delight in the Lord and He will give you your desires
Delight yourself in the Lord and he will give you the desires of your heart.

—PSALM 37:4

God satisfies the hungry and thirsty

He satisfies the thirsty and fills the hungry with good things.

—PSALM 107:9

Blessed are you who hunger now, for you will be satisfied. Blessed are you who weep now, for you will laugh.

—LUKE 6:21

Those who love the Lord are satisfied with longevity

With long life will I satisfy him and show him my salvation.

—PSALM 91:16

Savior

Jesus saves the lost

The Son of Man came to seek and to save what was lost.

—LUKE 19:10

Those who believe in Jesus receive eternal life

For God so loved the world that he gave his one and only Son, that whoever believes in him shall not perish but have eternal life.

—JOHN 3:16 (SEE ALSO JOHN 6:47)

Confess Jesus is Lord, and you'll be saved

If you confess with your mouth, "Jesus is Lord," and believe in your heart that God raised him from the dead, you will be saved.

— ROMANS 10:9

The Savior will return and transform us

Our citizenship is in heaven. And we eagerly await a Savior from there, the Lord Jesus Christ, who, by the power that enables him to bring everything under his control, will transform our lowly bodies so that they will be like his glorious body.

— PHILIPPIANS 3:20-21

Scripture

Scripture is inspired and leads us into truth

All Scripture is God-breathed and is useful for teaching, rebuking, correcting and training in righteousness, so that the man of God may be thoroughly equipped for every good work.

— 2 TIMOTHY 3:16-17

Obeying God's Word brings blessing

The man who looks intently into the perfect law that gives freedom, and continues to do this, not forgetting what he has heard, but doing it—he will be blessed in what he does.

— JAMES 1:25

Meditating on God's Word brings prosperity

Do not let this Book of the Law depart from your mouth;

meditate on it day and night, so that you may be careful to do everything written in it. Then you will be prosperous and successful.

—Joshua 1:8 (see also Psalm 1:1-3)

Those who love God's Word have peace
Great peace have they who love your law, and nothing can make them stumble.

—Psalm 119:165

Second Coming

Every eye will witness the Second Coming
Every eye will see him, even those who pierced him; and all the peoples of the earth will mourn because of him.

—Revelation 1:7

Christ will come suddenly
As lightning that comes from the east is visible even in the west, so will be the coming of the Son of Man.

—Matthew 24:27

The Lord will come at an unexpected hour
Therefore keep watch, because you do not know on what day your Lord will come.

—Matthew 24:42

Christ will come in great glory
At that time the sign of the Son of Man will appear in the sky, and all the nations of the earth will mourn. They will see the Son of Man coming on the clouds of the sky, with power and great glory.

— MATTHEW 24:30

Christians will receive a crown at the Second Coming
When the Chief Shepherd appears, you will receive the crown of glory that will never fade away.

— 1 PETER 5:4

Christ will come in judgment
Wait till the Lord comes. He will bring to light what is hidden in darkness and will expose the motives of men's hearts.

— 1 CORINTHIANS 4:5

Behold, I am coming soon! My reward is with me, and I will give to everyone according to what he has done.

— REVELATION 22:12 (SEE ALSO MATTHEW 16:27)

Security

Christ will never reject any who come to Him
All that the Father gives me will come to me, and whoever comes to me I will never drive away.

— JOHN 6:37

Our inheritance is secure

In his great mercy he has given us new birth into a living hope through the resurrection of Jesus Christ from the dead, and into an inheritance that can never perish, spoil or fade—kept in heaven for you.

— I PETER 1:3-4

The Holy Spirit guarantees our inheritance

It is God who makes both us and you stand firm in Christ. He anointed us, set his seal of ownership on us, and put his Spirit in our hearts as a deposit, guaranteeing what is to come.

— 2 CORINTHIANS 1:21-22

We are sealed by the Holy Spirit

Having believed, you were marked in him with a seal, the promised Holy Spirit, who is a deposit guaranteeing our inheritance until the redemption of those who are God's possession.

— EPHESIANS 1:13-14

Nothing can separate us from the love of God

I am convinced that neither death nor life, neither angels nor demons, neither the present nor the future, nor any powers, neither height nor depth, nor anything else in all creation, will be able to separate us from the love of God that is in Christ Jesus our Lord.

— ROMANS 8:38-39

We will not perish

I give them eternal life, and they shall never perish; no one can snatch them out of my hand.

— JOHN 10:28

Seeking God

The Lord is good to those who seek Him

The Lord is good to those whose hope is in him, to the one who seeks him.

— LAMENTATIONS 3:25

We find God when we seek Him with all our hearts

You will seek me and find me when you seek me with all your heart.

— JEREMIAH 29:13

God will draw near to those who draw near to Him

Come near to God and he will come near to you.

— JAMES 4:8

Those who seek the Lord find full satisfaction in Him

The lions may grow weak and hungry, but those who seek the Lord lack no good thing.

— PSALM 34:10

Self-Control

God can help you when you are tempted

Because he himself suffered when he was tempted, he is able to help those who are being tempted.

—HEBREWS 2:18

God can deliver you from any temptation

No temptation has seized you except what is common to man. And God is faithful; he will not let you be tempted beyond what you can bear. But when you are tempted, he will also provide a way out so that you can stand up under it.

—1 CORINTHIANS 10:13

Self-Denial

Whoever denies himself to follow Christ will find his life

If anyone would come after me, he must deny himself and take up his cross and follow me. For whoever wants to save his life will lose it, but whoever loses his life for me will find it.

—MATTHEW 16:24-25

If you put to death the misdeeds of the body, you will live

If you live according to the sinful nature, you will die; but if by the Spirit you put to death the misdeeds of the body, you will live.

—ROMANS 8:13

Seek God's kingdom first, and He will meet basic needs

Seek first his kingdom and his righteousness, and all these things will be given to you as well.

—MATTHEW 6:33

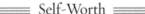

Self-Worth

We are of great worth to God

Are not two sparrows sold for a penny? Yet not one of them will fall to the ground apart from the will of your Father. And even the very hairs of your head are all numbered. So don't be afraid; you are worth more than many sparrows.

—MATTHEW 10:29-31

We are children of God

How great is the love the Father has lavished on us, that we should be called children of God! And that is what we are!

—1 JOHN 3:1

We are adopted into God's family

He predestined us to be adopted as his sons through Jesus Christ, in accordance with his pleasure and will—to the praise of his glorious grace, which he has freely given us in the One he loves.

—EPHESIANS 1:5-6 (SEE ALSO GALATIANS 3:26)

We are not slaves but children and heirs of God

Because you are sons, God sent the Spirit of his Son into our hearts, the Spirit who calls out, "Abba, Father." So you are no longer a slave, but a son; and since you are a son, God has made you also an heir.

—GALATIANS 4:6-7 (SEE ALSO ROMANS 8:14-15)

All people are equal in Christ

Here there is no Greek or Jew, circumcised or uncircumcised, barbarian, Scythian, slave or free, but Christ is all, and is in all.

—COLOSSIANS 3:11 (SEE ALSO GALATIANS 3:8)

Service

The Lord will reward our service

Whatever you do, work at it with all your heart, as working for the Lord, not for men, since you know that you will receive an inheritance from the Lord as a reward. It is the Lord Christ you are serving.

— COLOSSIANS 3:23-24

Even small acts of service bring blessing from God

If anyone gives even a cup of cold water to one of these little ones because he is my disciple, I tell you the truth, he will certainly not lose his reward.

— MATTHEW 10:42

We can comfort others

Praise be to the God and Father of our Lord Jesus Christ, the Father of compassion and the God of all comfort, who comforts us in all our troubles, so that we can comfort those in any trouble with the comfort we ourselves have received from God. For just as the sufferings of Christ flow over into our lives, so also through Christ our comfort overflows.

— 2 CORINTHIANS 1:3-5

Sexual Temptation

God can deliver you from any temptation

No temptation has seized you except what is common to man. And God is faithful; he will not let you be tempted beyond what you can bear. But when you are tempted, he will also provide a way out so that you can stand up under it.

— 1 CORINTHIANS 10:13

Dependence on the Holy Spirit brings victory

Live by the Spirit, and you will not gratify the desires of the sinful nature.

—GALATIANS 5:16

God will judge the sexually immoral

Marriage should be honored by all, and the marriage bed kept pure, for God will judge the adulterer and all the sexually immoral.

—HEBREWS 13:4

The Lord knows how to rescue godly men

The Lord knows how to rescue godly men from trials.

—2 PETER 2:9

Sickness

The prayer of faith will make a sick person well

Is any one of you sick? He should call the elders of the church to pray over him and anoint him with oil in the name of the Lord. And the prayer offered in faith will make the sick person well; the Lord will raise him up.

—JAMES 5:14-15

Though outwardly wasting away, we are inwardly renewed

We do not lose heart. Though outwardly we are wasting away, yet inwardly we are being renewed day by day.

—2 CORINTHIANS 4:16

Permanent resurrection bodies await us

We know that if the earthly tent we live in is destroyed, we have a building from God, an eternal house in heaven, not built by human hands.

— 2 Corinthians 5:1

Sin

We are forgiven of our sins

In him we have redemption through his blood, the forgiveness of sins, in accordance with the riches of God's grace.

— Ephesians 1:7 (see also Colossians 2:13-14; Matthew 26:28)

God blots out our transgressions

I, even I, am he who blots out your transgressions, for my own sake, and remembers your sins no more.

— Isaiah 43:25

God cleanses the stain of sin from your soul

"Come now, let us reason together," says the Lord. "Though your sins are like scarlet, they shall be as white as snow; though they are red as crimson, they shall be like wool."

— Isaiah 1:18

If we do sin, Jesus is our advocate

I write this to you so that you will not sin. But if anybody does sin, we have one who speaks to the Father in our defense—Jesus Christ, the Righteous One. He is the atoning sacrifice for our sins, and not only for ours but also for the sins of the whole world.

—1 JOHN 2:1-2

God cleanses us of sins when we confess to Him

If we confess our sins, he is faithful and just and will forgive us our sins and purify us from all unrighteousness.

—1 JOHN 1:9

Slander

Those persecuted for righteousness' sake are blessed

Blessed are those who are persecuted because of righteousness, for theirs is the kingdom of heaven.

—MATTHEW 5:10

Those persecuted for following Jesus are blessed

Blessed are you when people insult you, persecute you and falsely say all kinds of evil against you because of me. Rejoice and be glad, because great is your reward in heaven.

—MATTHEW 5:11-12

Spiritual Recovery

God gives strength to the weary

He gives strength to the weary and increases the power of the weak.

—ISAIAH 40:29

Christ gives us rest

Come to me, all you who are weary and burdened, and I will give you rest.

— MATTHEW 11:28

The Lord renews our strength

Even youths grow tired and weary, and young men stumble and fall; but those who hope in the Lord will renew their strength. They will soar on wings like eagles; they will run and not grow weary, they will walk and not be faint.

— ISAIAH 40:30-31

We are inwardly renewed daily

We do not lose heart. Though outwardly we are wasting away, yet inwardly we are being renewed day by day. For our light and momentary troubles are achieving for us an eternal glory that far outweighs them all. So we fix our eyes not on what is seen, but on what is unseen. For what is seen is temporary, but what is unseen is eternal.

— 2 CORINTHIANS 4:16-18

Stability

God stabilizes the lives of those who delight in Him

If the Lord delights in a man's way, he makes his steps firm;

though he stumble, he will not fall, for the Lord upholds him with his hand.

—PSALM 37:23-24

The one who loves does not stumble
Whoever loves his brother lives in the light, and there is nothing in him to make him stumble.

—1 JOHN 2:10

Strength

Christ gives us strength for all things
I can do everything through him who gives me strength.

—PHILIPPIANS 4:13

God's power is made perfect in weakness
My grace is sufficient for you, for my power is made perfect in weakness.

—2 CORINTHIANS 12:9

The Lord renews our strength
Those who hope in the Lord will renew their strength. They will soar on wings like eagles; they will run and not grow weary, they will walk and not be faint.

—ISAIAH 40:31

God is our strength
God is our refuge and strength, an ever-present help in trouble.

—PSALM 46:1

God will strengthen us
My hand will sustain him; surely my arm will strengthen him.

—PSALM 89:21

God gives strength to the weary
He gives strength to the weary and increases the power of the weak.

—ISAIAH 40:29 (SEE ALSO PSALM 29:11; 2 THESSALONIANS 3:3)

Stress

Turning anxieties over to God yields perfect peace
Do not be anxious about anything, but in everything, by prayer and petition, with thanksgiving, present your requests to God. And the peace of God, which transcends all understanding, will guard your hearts and your minds in Christ Jesus.

—PHILIPPIANS 4:6-7

God is with you
Do not fear, for I am with you; do not be dismayed, for I am

your God. I will strengthen you and help you; I will uphold you with my righteous right hand.

—ISAIAH 41:10

You can cast your anxieties on God
Cast all your anxiety on him because he cares for you.

—1 PETER 5:7

Christ gives us peace
Peace I leave with you; my peace I give you. I do not give to you as the world gives. Do not let your hearts be troubled and do not be afraid.

—JOHN 14:27

Success

The one who delights in God's Word succeeds
Blessed is the man who does not walk in the counsel of the wicked or stand in the way of sinners or sit in the seat of mockers. But his delight is in the law of the Lord, and on his law he meditates day and night. He is like a tree planted by streams of water, which yields its fruit in season and whose leaf does not wither. Whatever he does prospers.

—PSALM 1:1-3

The one who meditates on God's Word succeeds
Do not let this Book of the Law depart from your mouth;

meditate on it day and night, so that you may be careful to do everything written in it. Then you will be prosperous and successful.

—JOSHUA 1:8

Suffering

God delivers us from troubles

A righteous man may have many troubles, but the Lord delivers him from them all.

—PSALM 34:19

Christ our comfort overflows in our lives

Just as the sufferings of Christ flow over into our lives, so also through Christ our comfort overflows.

—2 CORINTHIANS 1:5

God brings restoration

The God of all grace, who called you to his eternal glory in Christ, after you have suffered a little while, will himself restore you and make you strong, firm and steadfast.

—1 PETER 5:10

We participate in the sufferings of Christ

Do not be surprised at the painful trial you are suffering, as though something strange were happening to you. But rejoice that you participate in the sufferings of Christ, so that you may be overjoyed when his glory is revealed.

—1 PETER 4:12-13 (SEE ALSO ROMANS 8:16-17)

God uses hardship to discipline us

The Lord disciplines those he loves, and he punishes everyone he accepts as a son. Endure hardship as discipline; God is treating you as sons.

—HEBREWS 12:6-7

Our present sufferings pale in comparison to our future glory

I consider that our present sufferings are not worth comparing with the glory that will be revealed in us.

—ROMANS 8:18

═══════════ Sufficiency of Jesus ═══════════

God will meet all our needs in Jesus

My God will meet all your needs according to his glorious riches in Christ Jesus.

—PHILIPPIANS 4:19

We can do all things through Christ who gives us strength

I can do everything through him who gives me strength.

—PHILIPPIANS 4:13

We have spiritual blessings in Christ

Praise be to the God and Father of our Lord Jesus Christ,

who has blessed us in the heavenly realms with every spiritual blessing in Christ.

—EPHESIANS 1:3

Jesus sets us free

If the Son sets you free, you will be free indeed.

—JOHN 8:36

Jesus' strength is made perfect in human weakness

My grace is sufficient for you, for my power is made perfect in weakness.

—2 CORINTHIANS 12:9

Those who believe in Jesus are spiritually satisfied

Jesus declared, "I am the bread of life. He who comes to me will never go hungry, and he who believes in me will never be thirsty."

—JOHN 6:35

Supplication

Ask and it will be given to you

Ask and it will be given to you; seek and you will find; knock and the door will be opened to you. For everyone who asks receives; he who seeks finds; and to him who knocks, the door will be opened.

—MATTHEW 7:7-8 (SEE ALSO LUKE 11:9-11)

God answers prayer when we believe
If you believe, you will receive whatever you ask for in prayer.

—MATTHEW 21:22

God answers prayer when we abide in Christ
If you remain in me and my words remain in you, ask whatever you wish, and it will be given you.

—JOHN 15:7

God answers prayer when two or more agree
If two of you on earth agree about anything you ask for, it will be done for you by my Father in heaven. For where two or three come together in my name, there am I with them.

—MATTHEW 18:19-20

God answers prayer when we pray in Jesus' name
Until now you have not asked for anything in my name. Ask and you will receive, and your joy will be complete.

—JOHN 16:24 (SEE ALSO JOHN 14:13-14)

T

God can deliver you from any temptation

No temptation has seized you except what is common to man. And God is faithful; he will not let you be tempted beyond what you can bear. But when you are tempted, he will also provide a way out so that you can stand up under it.

—1 Corinthians 10:13

Dependence on the Spirit brings victory

Live by the Spirit, and you will not gratify the desires of the sinful nature.

—Galatians 5:16

Jesus helps us in our temptations

Because he himself suffered when he was tempted, he is able to help those who are being tempted.

—Hebrews 2:18

The Lord knows how to rescue godly men

The Lord knows how to rescue godly men from trials.

— 2 PETER 2:9

Jesus is sympathetic with our weaknesses and can help us

We do not have a high priest who is unable to sympathize with our weaknesses, but we have one who has been tempted in every way, just as we are—yet was without sin. Let us then approach the throne of grace with confidence, so that we may receive mercy and find grace to help us in our time of need.

— HEBREWS 4:15-16

We are conquerors through Jesus

In all these things we are more than conquerors through him who loved us.

— ROMANS 8:37

Tongue

Every tongue will confess Jesus as Lord

God exalted him to the highest place and gave him the name that is above every name, that at the name of Jesus every knee should bow, in heaven and on earth and under the earth, and every tongue confess that Jesus Christ is Lord, to the glory of God the Father.

— PHILIPPIANS 2:9-11

Transformation

We are being molded in Christ's image

We, who with unveiled faces all reflect the Lord's glory, are being transformed into his likeness with ever-increasing glory, which comes from the Lord, who is the Spirit.

— 2 CORINTHIANS 3:18

We are transformed by the renewing of our minds

Do not conform any longer to the pattern of this world, but be transformed by the renewing of your mind. Then you will be able to test and approve what God's will is—his good, pleasing and perfect will.

— ROMANS 12:2

God continues to do His work in us

He who began a good work in you will carry it on to completion until the day of Christ Jesus.

— PHILIPPIANS 1:6

Jesus will transform our lowly bodies to be glorious bodies

Our citizenship is in heaven. And we eagerly await a Savior from there, the Lord Jesus Christ, who, by the power that enables him to bring everything under his control, will transform our lowly bodies so that they will be like his glorious body.

— PHILIPPIANS 3:20-21

Trials

The Lord knows how to rescue godly men from trials
The Lord knows how to rescue godly men from trials.

—2 PETER 2:9

The Lord delivers us from troubles
The righteous cry out, and the Lord hears them; he delivers them from all their troubles.

—PSALM 34:17

The Lord will sustain us in our troubles
Cast your cares on the Lord and he will sustain you; he will never let the righteous fall.

—PSALM 55:22

Persevere, and you'll receive the crown of life
Blessed is the man who perseveres under trial, because when he has stood the test, he will receive the crown of life that God has promised to those who love him.

—JAMES 1:12

Christ gives us rest
Come to me, all you who are weary and burdened, and I will give you rest.

—MATTHEW 11:28

Trouble

The Lord is a refuge in times of trouble

The Lord is good, a refuge in times of trouble. He cares for those who trust in him.

—NAHUM 1:7 (SEE ALSO PSALM 9:9)

The Lord delivers the righteous from their troubles

The righteous cry out, and the Lord hears them; he delivers them from all their troubles. The Lord is close to the broken-hearted and saves those who are crushed in spirit.

—PSALM 34:17-18

God comforts us in all our troubles

Praise be to the God and Father of our Lord Jesus Christ, the Father of compassion and the God of all comfort, who comforts us in all our troubles, so that we can comfort those in any trouble with the comfort we ourselves have received from God.

—2 CORINTHIANS 1:3-4

If we call upon God, He will deliver us from our troubles

Call upon me in the day of trouble; I will deliver you, and you will honor me.

—PSALM 50:15

Even in our troubles, God is working for our good

We know that in all things God works for the good of

those who love him, who have been called according to his purpose.

—ROMANS 8:28

Christ has overcome the world, and in Him we have peace

I have told you these things, so that in me you may have peace. In this world you will have trouble. But take heart! I have overcome the world.

—JOHN 16:33

Our momentary troubles are achieving great glory for us

Our light and momentary troubles are achieving for us an eternal glory that far outweighs them all. So we fix our eyes not on what is seen, but on what is unseen. For what is seen is temporary, but what is unseen is eternal.

—2 CORINTHIANS 4:17-18

Trust

God cares for those who trust in Him

The Lord is good, a refuge in times of trouble. He cares for those who trust in him.

—NAHUM 1:7

The man who trusts the Lord is blessed

Blessed is the man who trusts in the Lord, whose confidence is in him.

—JEREMIAH 17:7

Blessed is the man who makes the Lord his trust, who does not look to the proud, to those who turn aside to false gods.

—PSALM 40:4

The Lord's love surrounds the one who trusts in Him

Many are the woes of the wicked, but the Lord's unfailing love surrounds the man who trusts in him.

—PSALM 32:10

Peace accompanies the one who trusts in God

You will keep in perfect peace him whose mind is steadfast, because he trusts in you. Trust in the Lord forever, for the Lord, the Lord, is the Rock eternal.

—ISAIAH 26:3-4

Truth

The Spirit of truth guides us into all truth

When he, the Spirit of truth, comes, he will guide you into all truth.

—JOHN 16:13

God's Word provides us truth

The law of the Lord is perfect, reviving the soul. The statutes of the Lord are trustworthy, making wise the simple. The precepts of the Lord are right, giving joy to the heart. The commands of the Lord are radiant, giving light to the eyes. The fear of the Lord is pure, enduring forever. The ordinances of the Lord are sure and altogether righteous.

—PSALM 19:7-9

The truth sets us free

You will know the truth, and the truth will set you free.

—JOHN 8:32

The Lord is near to those who call on Him in truth

The Lord is near to all who call on him, to all who call on him in truth.

—PSALM 145:18

U-V

We are conquerors in Christ
In all these things we are more than conquerors through him who loved us.

—ROMANS 8:37

We have peace in Jesus the Conqueror
I have told you these things, so that in me you may have peace. In this world you will have trouble. But take heart! I have overcome the world.

—JOHN 16:33

With God we will gain the victory
With God we will gain the victory, and he will trample down our enemies.

—PSALM 60:12

Everyone born of God overcomes the world
Everyone born of God overcomes the world. This is the victory that has overcome the world, even our faith. Who is it

242

that overcomes the world? Only he who believes that Jesus is the Son of God.

—1 John 5:4-5

God will crush Satan
The God of peace will soon crush Satan under your feet.

—Romans 16:20

Death will be swallowed up in victory
When the perishable has been clothed with the imperishable, and the mortal with immortality, then the saying that is written will come true: "Death has been swallowed up in victory."

—1 Corinthians 15:54

W-X-Y-Z

===== Waiting on God =====

The Savior will return and transform us

Our citizenship is in heaven. And we eagerly await a Savior from there, the Lord Jesus Christ, who, by the power that enables him to bring everything under his control, will transform our lowly bodies so that they will be like his glorious body.

— PHILIPPIANS 3:20-21

Blessed are all who wait for God

The Lord longs to be gracious to you; he rises to show you compassion. For the Lord is a God of justice. Blessed are all who wait for him!

— ISAIAH 30:18

The Lord is good to those who wait on Him

The Lord is good to those whose hope is in him, to the one who seeks him; it is good to wait quietly for the salvation of the Lord.

— LAMENTATIONS 3:25-26

Christ will bring final salvation to those who wait for Him

Christ was sacrificed once to take away the sins of many people; and he will appear a second time, not to bear sin, but to bring salvation to those who are waiting for him.

—HEBREWS 9:28

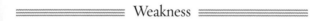

Weakness

God increases the power of the weak

He gives strength to the weary and increases the power of the weak.

—ISAIAH 40:29

God's power is made perfect in weakness

My grace is sufficient for you, for my power is made perfect in weakness.

—2 CORINTHIANS 12:9

Christ sympathizes with our weaknesses

We do not have a high priest who is unable to sympathize with our weaknesses, but we have one who has been tempted in every way, just as we are—yet was without sin.

—HEBREWS 4:15

245

The Spirit helps us in our weakness

The Spirit himself intercedes for us with groans that words cannot express.

—ROMANS 8:26

God blesses those who help the weak

Blessed is he who has regard for the weak; the Lord delivers him in times of trouble. The Lord will protect him and preserve his life.

—PSALM 41:1-2

Will of God

God will guide us

I will instruct you and teach you in the way you should go; I will counsel you and watch over you.

—PSALM 32:8

God gives us wisdom if we ask in faith

If any of you lacks wisdom, he should ask God, who gives generously to all without finding fault, and it will be given to him.

—JAMES 1:5

Minds transformed by God's Word can discern His will

Do not conform any longer to the pattern of this world, but

be transformed by the renewing of your mind. Then you will be able to test and approve what God's will is—his good, pleasing and perfect will.

—ROMANS 12:2

The Lord makes our steps firm
If the Lord delights in a man's way, he makes his steps firm.

—PSALM 37:23

God is our guide to the very end of our lives
This God is our God for ever and ever; he will be our guide even to the end.

—PSALM 48:14

Wisdom

God gives wisdom to those who ask in faith
If any of you lacks wisdom, he should ask God, who gives generously to all without finding fault, and it will be given to him.

—JAMES 1:5

God is a rich store of wisdom
He will be the sure foundation for your times, a rich store of salvation and wisdom and knowledge; the fear of the Lord is the key to this treasure.

—ISAIAH 33:6

God's Word makes us wise

The law of the Lord is perfect, reviving the soul. The statutes of the Lord are trustworthy, making wise the simple. The precepts of the Lord are right, giving joy to the heart. The commands of the Lord are radiant, giving light to the eyes.

—PSALM 19:7-8

Scripture is inspired and thoroughly equips us

All Scripture is God-breathed and is useful for teaching, rebuking, correcting and training in righteousness, so that the man of God may be thoroughly equipped for every good work.

—2 TIMOTHY 3:16-17

Hearing God's Word increases our faith

Faith comes from hearing the message, and the message is heard through the word of Christ.

—ROMANS 10:17

Meditating on God's Word leads to prosperity

Do not let this Book of the Law depart from your mouth; meditate on it day and night, so that you may be careful to do everything written in it. Then you will be prosperous and successful.

—JOSHUA 1:8

Being doers of the Word brings blessing

Do not merely listen to the word, and so deceive yourselves. Do what it says. Anyone who listens to the word but does not do what it says is like a man who looks at his face in a mirror and, after looking at himself, goes away and immediately forgets what he looks like. But the man who looks intently into the perfect law that gives freedom, and continues to do this, not forgetting what he has heard, but doing it—he will be blessed in what he does.

—JAMES 1:22-25

God's Word stands forever

The grass withers and the flowers fall, but the word of our God stands forever.

—ISAIAH 40:8 (SEE ALSO 1 PETER 1:23-25)

Work

Our work will be rewarded

Whatever you do, work at it with all your heart, as working for the Lord, not for men, since you know that you will receive an inheritance from the Lord as a reward. It is the Lord Christ you are serving.

—COLOSSIANS 3:23-24

Your labor is not in vain

Let nothing move you. Always give yourselves fully to the work of the Lord, because you know that your labor in the Lord is not in vain.

—1 CORINTHIANS 15:58

God gives you what you need to do every good work

God is able to make all grace abound to you, so that in all things at all times, having all that you need, you will abound in every good work.

—2 CORINTHIANS 9:8

Christ gives rest to the overworked

Come to me, all you who are weary and burdened, and I will give you rest.

—MATTHEW 11:28

World

You need not be conformed to this world

Do not conform any longer to the pattern of this world, but be transformed by the renewing of your mind. Then you will be able to test and approve what God's will is—his good, pleasing and perfect will.

—ROMANS 12:2

Those who do the will of God live forever

Do not love the world or anything in the world. If anyone loves
the world, the love of the Father is not in him. For everything
in the world—the cravings of sinful man, the lust of his eyes
and the boasting of what he has and does—comes not from
the Father but from the world. The world and its desires pass
away, but the man who does the will of God lives forever.

—1 JOHN 2:15-17

Heavenly treasures cannot be lost

Do not store up for yourselves treasures on earth, where moth
and rust destroy, and where thieves break in and steal. But
store up for yourselves treasures in heaven, where moth and
rust do not destroy, and where thieves do not break in and
steal. For where your treasure is, there your heart will be also.

—MATTHEW 6:19-21

Jesus is the light of the world

I have come into the world as a light, so that no one who
believes in me should stay in darkness.

—JOHN 12:46

Christ has overcome the world, and in Him we have peace

I have told you these things, so that in me you may have
peace. In this world you will have trouble. But take heart! I
have overcome the world.

—JOHN 16:33

Worry

Turning anxieties over to God yields perfect peace

Do not be anxious about anything, but in everything, by prayer and petition, with thanksgiving, present your requests to God. And the peace of God, which transcends all understanding, will guard your hearts and your minds in Christ Jesus.

—PHILIPPIANS 4:6-7

The Lord sustains us in our troubles

Cast your cares on the Lord and he will sustain you; he will never let the righteous fall.

—PSALM 55:22

God will meet all our needs

My God will meet all your needs according to his glorious riches in Christ Jesus.

—PHILIPPIANS 4:19

God is our refuge and strength

God is our refuge and strength, an ever-present help in trouble.

—PSALM 46:1

Christ gives us peace

Peace I leave with you; my peace I give you. I do not give to you as the world gives. Do not let your hearts be troubled and do not be afraid.

—JOHN 14:27

The mind focused on God is in perfect peace
You will keep in perfect peace him whose mind is steadfast, because he trusts in you. Trust in the Lord forever, for the Lord, the Lord, is the Rock eternal.

—ISAIAH 26:3-4

God's Covenant Promises

A covenant is a promise-agreement between two parties. A covenant is a special kind of foundational promise. Covenants were used among the ancients in the form of treaties or alliances between nations (1 Samuel 11:1), treaties between individual people (Genesis 21:27), friendship pacts (1 Samuel 18:3), and agreements between God and His people.

In the Bible, God made specific covenant promises to a number of people, including Noah (Genesis 9:8-17), Abraham (Genesis 15:12-21; 17:1-14), the Israelites at Mount Sinai (Exodus 19:5-6), David (2 Samuel 7:13; 23:5), and God's people in the New Covenant (Hebrews 8:6-13). In what follows, I will summarize the more important of these covenants.

1. Abrahamic Covenant. A very famous covenant is God's covenant with Abraham (Genesis 12:1-3; 15:18-21), which was later reaffirmed with Isaac (17:21) and Jacob (35:10-12). In this covenant, God promised to make Abraham's descendants His own special people. More specifically, God promised Abraham: 1) I will make you a great nation; 2) I will bless you; 3) I will make your name great; 4) You will be a blessing; 5) I will bless those who bless you; 6) I will curse those who curse you; and 7) All peoples on earth will be blessed through you.

These covenant promises were unconditional in nature. A

conditional covenant is a covenant with an "if" attached. This type of covenant demanded that the people meet certain obligations or conditions before God was obligated to fulfill that which was promised. If God's people failed in meeting the conditions, God was not obligated in any way to fulfill the promise.

As opposed to this, an *unconditional* covenant depended on no such conditions for its fulfillment. There were no "ifs" attached. That which was promised was sovereignly given to the recipient of the covenant apart from any merit (or lack thereof) on the part of the recipient. The covenant God made with Abraham was unconditional.

The promises God made to Abraham must have seemed incredible. After all, God promised him that his descendants would be as numerous as the stars in the sky (Genesis 12:1-3; 13:14-17). The promise must have seemed unbelievable to Abraham since his wife was childless (11:30). Yet Abraham did not doubt God; he knew God would faithfully give what He had promised. God even reaffirmed the covenant in Genesis 15, perhaps to emphasize to Abraham that even in his advanced age, the promise would come to pass.

At one point, an impatient Sarah suggested that their heir might be procured through their Egyptian handmaiden, Hagar. Ishmael was thus born to Abraham, through Hagar, when he was 86 years old. But Ishmael was not the child of promise. In God's perfect timing, the child of promise was finally born when Abraham and Sarah were very old (Abraham was 100), far beyond normal childbearing age.

They named their son Isaac (Genesis 21), and, as promised, an entire nation eventually developed from his line. Isaac means "laughter" and is a fitting name because it points to the joy derived from this child of promise.

2. Davidic Covenant. God later made a covenant with David in which He promised that one of his descendants would rule forever (2 Samuel 7:12-13; 22:51). This is another example of an unconditional covenant. It did not depend on David in any way for its fulfillment. David realized this when he received the promise from God, and responded with an attitude of humility and a recognition of God's sovereignty over the affairs of men. This covenant finds its ultimate fulfillment in Jesus Christ, who was born from the line of David (Matthew 1:1).

3. Sinai Covenant. God's covenant with Israel at Mount Sinai, following Israel's sojourn through the wilderness after being delivered from Egypt, constituted the formal basis of the redemptive relationship between God and the Israelites (Exodus 19:3-25). This covenant was couched in terms of ancient Hittite suzerainty treaties made between kings and their subjects. Such treaties would always include a preamble naming the author of the treaty, a historical introduction depicting the relationship between the respective parties, a list of stipulations explaining the responsibilities of each of the parties, a promise of either blessing or judgment invoked depending on faithfulness or unfaithfulness to the treaty, a solemn oath, and a religious ratification of the treaty. In such treaties, the motivation for obedience to the stipulations was the undeserved favor of the king making the treaty. Out of gratitude, the people were to obey the stipulations.

Such parallels between ancient treaties and God's covenant with Israel show that God communicated to His people in ways they were familiar with. Key parallels between such treaties and the Sinai Covenant are that God gave stipulations to the people explaining their responsibilities (the law, Exodus 20:1-17) and gave a promise of blessing for obeying the law and a promise of judgment for disobeying the law (see Exodus 19:5-8; 24:3,7). Sadly, Israel was often disobedient to God's covenant (Exodus 32:1-31; Jeremiah 31:32). In this covenant, blessing was conditioned on obedience.

Old Testament history is replete with illustrations of how unfaithful Israel was to the covenant. The two most significant periods of exile for the Jewish people involved the fall of Israel to the Assyrians in 722 BC and the collapse of Judah under Babylonian siege in 597-581 BC. As God promised, disobedience brought exile to God's own people.

The first chapter of Isaiah takes the form of a lawsuit against Judah. Judah was indicted by the Lord (through Isaiah) because of Judah's "breach of contract" in breaking the Sinai Covenant, which had been given to the nation at the time of the Exodus from Egypt. In this courtroom scene, the Lord called upon heaven and earth to act as witnesses to the accusations leveled against the nation (Isaiah 1:2). The whole universe was to bear witness that God's judgments are just.

The Lord indicted Judah for rebelling against Him. The Hebrew word for "rebel" in Isaiah 1:2 was often used among the ancients in reference to a subordinate state's violation of treaty with a sovereign nation. In Isaiah 1, the word points to Judah's blatant violation of God's covenant. Therefore, Israel went into captivity.

In this case, the Babylonian captivity was God's means of chastening Judah. Of course, God intended this judgment to be corrective. Throughout both the Old and New Testaments, we find that God disciplines His children to purify them. Just as an earthly father disciplines his children, so God the Father disciplines His children to train and educate them (Hebrews 12:1-6).

4. The New Covenant. The New Covenant is an unconditional covenant God made with humankind in which He promised to provide for forgiveness of sin, based entirely on the sacrificial death and resurrection of Jesus Christ (Jeremiah 31:31-34). Under the Old Covenant, worshipers never enjoyed a sense of total forgiveness. Under the New Covenant, however, Christ our High Priest made provision for such forgiveness. When Jesus ate the Passover meal with the disciples in the Upper Room, He spoke of the cup as "the new covenant in my blood" (Luke 22:20; see also 1 Corinthians 11:25). Jesus has done all that is necessary for the forgiveness of sins by His once-and-for-all sacrifice on the cross. This New Covenant is the basis for our relationship with God in the New Testament.

Resources

The following resources were very helpful in deriving insights on Greek and Hebrew words and collecting quotes:

Books

1. *Draper's Book of Quotations for the Christian World* (Grand Rapids, MI: Baker Book House, 1992).

2. William MacDonald, *Believer's Bible Commentary* (Nashville, TN: Thomas Nelson Publishers, 1995).

3. Larry Richards, *Every Promise in the Bible* (Nashville, TN: Thomas Nelson Publishing, 1998).

Software

1. Accordance Bible Software, published by Oaksoft Software

2. HyperCard stack, published by Apple Computer, Inc.

3. Sage Digital Library, published by Sage Software

Websites

1. <www.cyberhymnal.org>

══ More Great Harvest House Books ══
About the Promises of God

One-Minute Promises

Steve Miller

This gathering of *One-Minute Promises* provides the assurances of faith in brief, inspirational meditations. You will experience the abundance that comes when you place hope in God's promises every day.

One-Minute Promises of Comfort

Steve Miller

Resting in God's promises provides great solace, renewal, and hope when you must undergo a trial. This collection of promises gives you biblical assurance of God's presence and guidance, unveiling God's power to transform your life.

Walking in God's Promises

Elizabeth George

Exploring Sarah's life—her difficult circumstances and mistakes—you will learn to let God stretch and shape you. You will also learn to trust in His promises. Questions, Bible study tips, and a "heart response" for personal application are all included.

Powerful Promises for Every Woman

Elizabeth George

Through His promises, God's guidance never falters. Bestselling author Elizabeth George teaches you about 12 promises listed in Psalm 23, including provision, healing, and protection. You will gain joy and comfort in your journey.